You're
Worth
MORE
Than You
Think!

The Riverboat Adventures

1. *Escape Into the Night*
2. *Race for Freedom*
3. *Midnight Rescue*
4. *The Swindler's Treasure*
5. *Mysterious Signal*
6. *The Fiddler's Secret*

Adventures of the Northwoods

1. *The Disappearing Stranger*
2. *The Hidden Message*
3. *The Creeping Shadows*
4. *The Vanishing Footprints*
5. *Trouble at Wild River*
6. *The Mysterious Hideaway*
7. *Grandpa's Stolen Treasure*
8. *The Runaway Clown*
9. *Mystery of the Missing Map*
10. *Disaster on Windy Hill*

Let's-Talk-About-It Stories for Kids

1. *You're Worth More Than You Think!*
2. *Secrets of the Best Choice*

LET'S TALK ABOUT IT
STORIES FOR Kids

You're Worth MORE Than You Think!

LOIS WALFRID JOHNSON

BETHANY HOUSE PUBLISHERS
MINNEAPOLIS, MINNESOTA 55438

Published by Bethany House Publishers
A Ministry of Bethany Fellowship International
11400 Hampshire Avenue South
Minneapolis, Minnesota 55438
www.bethanyhouse.com

Printed in the United States of America by
Bethany Press International, Minneapolis, Minnesota 55438

ISBN 1-55661-651-1

To Ken and Claire Wesloh
and
to every person
who has prayed for my writing

You're worth more than you know
in the Father's eyes and in mine

LOIS WALFRID JOHNSON is the bestselling author of more than twenty-five books. Her work has been translated into twelve languages and has received many awards, including the Gold Medallion, the C. S. Lewis Silver Medal, the Wisconsin State Historical Society Award, and five Silver Angels from Excellence in Media. Yet Lois believes that one of her greatest rewards is knowing that readers enjoy her books.

In all that she does, Lois seeks to live what she believes. She and her husband, Roy, are former teachers and have used the principles Lois writes about with their own children and the children they've taught. The Johnsons presently make their home in Minnesota.

To the Kids Who Read This Book

Have you ever faced something you thought you couldn't do? Did it seem so difficult that you felt you were fighting a lion or bear? Maybe you wondered, *How can I possibly win?*

You might feel that way right now. You tell yourself, *I'm not good enough. I'll never make it. I can't do it.*

It's easy to think that you're not up to doing everything you'd like. But there's another way—one that a young boy named David knew.

David had some hard things to face. Everything didn't go the way he wanted. Though he was still a boy, he had a tough job. To save his father's sheep, David had to kill lions and bears. Then God sent him to fight a giant!

Goliath was a nine-foot-tall soldier in the Philistine army. Morning and evening for forty days he shouted threats to the army of Israel, God's chosen nation. "Choose one of your men to fight me!" the giant yelled. "If he kills me, we'll be your slaves. If I kill him, you'll be *our* slaves!"

Goliath was the world's biggest bully. He even frightened Saul, the king of Israel, and his soldiers. As they listened to the giant's threats, men who were used to fighting became afraid to fight back. But when David heard Goliath's words, he asked, "Who is this Philistine that threatens the army of the living God?"

David's older brother made fun of him, saying, "Who do you think *you* are?"

Then King Saul told David, "You're only a boy. Goliath has been a soldier all his life!"

Yet David took his slingshot, collected five stones from the creek, and started toward the giant.

Goliath also saw that David was only a boy. The giant poked fun at David. "Come here!" he roared. "I'll give your body to the birds and animals to eat!"

"You come against me with a sword and a spear," David shouted back. "But I come against you in the name of the Lord Almighty, the God of the armies of Israel! It's not by sword or spear that the Lord saves, for the battle is the Lord's!"

Goliath moved closer, and David ran forward to meet him. Hurling a stone from his sling, he struck Goliath on the forehead.

The giant fell facedown on the ground. Then David took Goliath's own sword and killed him.

When you think about David, you may tell yourself, "I couldn't do what he did."

That's right, you couldn't. God hasn't asked you to kill Goliath. But God knows that you face other giants. And God gave David a secret source of power—His Holy Spirit.

David didn't trust in what *he* could do. Instead, he knew God and knew what God could do *for* him. Because of that, David had a godly self-esteem.

Self-esteem isn't the feeling that you're better than everyone else. Nor is it the belief that your way is always best. Self-esteem is not even thinking that you deserve the best, or at least whatever you want. **Godly self-esteem means having a healthy respect for yourself because of what God thinks about you.**

If you don't like yourself, it's hard to love and help others. You feel as weak as a newborn puppy needing milk to stay alive. **But when you have godly self-esteem, you know that God loves you and that you belong to Him.** You know you are valuable just the way you are. You believe you have something to offer others.

The stories in this book show kids who face the kinds of problems you know about. These boys and girls need to make choices—whether to lose their battles or accept God's help and win. They need to decide whether they'll become like David—an in-spite-of-it kid with Holy Spirit power.

As you read the stories, put yourself in their gym shoes. Ask, *What would I do if this were happening to me or one of my friends?* Talk with someone special about the questions at the end of each story.

You'll see new ways of making choices. You'll think about how to deal with things that bother you. Then turn the book upside down. Repeat the Bible verse to yourself until you receive the help it gives. Say the prayer, or pray in your own words. Learn to believe in a powerful God.

You'll catch on to something big. **It helps to use the Bible in your choices.** Often there's a story or verse that fits exactly what you need to know. Other times it's important to think about the overall teaching of the Bible. For instance, God tells us to love one another. If you wonder about doing something, ask yourself, *Would it* help *someone (show love)? Or would it* hurt *that person?*

You may already have learned to ask the question, *What would Jesus do?* Take the next step. Pray, *Jesus, what do you want* me *to do? How do you want me to follow* you?

If Jesus is the most important Person in your life, you won't be stopped by the hard things you face. You'll keep on in spite of the things that hurt you or make you afraid. But you need to be honest with Jesus and tell Him right up front, "I need your help." And because you ask for His help, you'll get it.

When a pro baseball player comes to bat, he isn't looking around at the stands. He keeps his eyes on the ball. In the same way, **keep your eyes on Jesus. In everything you do, He is the audience you care about. He is the one who will help you.**

God the Father created you. His Son, Jesus, loves you so much that He died for you. The Holy Spirit wants to give you courage and the power and help you need. To them you are worth more than you can even guess.

You're worth more than you think!

The Long Swim

As Mickey peered out the window, his dad backed into a camping spot. Around the car, pine trees formed a windbreak for the tent they would pitch. Far below, the waves of the Pacific Ocean pounded against a sandy beach.

"Everybody out!" Dad said. "As soon as we're set up, you can swim."

Mickey followed his older brother, Troy, from the car and helped Mom take out the food. While she spread a cloth on the picnic table, Mickey set a cake on the bench. Dad and Troy lifted the tent and stakes from the trunk.

As soon as Troy checked over the campsite, he started telling Mickey what to do. "Spread out the ground tarp. Get the hammer." Then, "Hold the stake on that side while I pound one in over here."

At first Mickey didn't mind. Troy always got things done. *I wish I could be like him,* Mickey thought, as he often had before. Besides, the quicker they did the work, the longer they'd have to swim.

But as soon as the tent was up, Troy gave more orders. "I saw the pump that way." Tossing Mickey two large jugs, he pointed toward a path.

Still looking forward to being in the ocean, Mickey set out quickly. He liked to swim, and it was the one thing he could do better than Troy. Mickey practiced more and learned new strokes by watching older kids.

Even so, as he started back with the water, he walked slower. *Why does Troy always have to be the boss?*

The trail led uphill, and the jugs got heavier with each step. As they bumped against his knees, Mickey grew hot and sweaty. *This is hard,* he thought. *Why couldn't Troy do it?*

As Mickey drew near the campsite, he heard Dad call out to his brother. "Good job, Troy! We're setting up in less time every day."

Mickey knew Dad was right. Troy *had* done a good job. But Mickey felt an uneasy twinge. Somehow he felt worthless—as though he could never measure up.

When he came into the clearing, he tried to carry the jugs the way Troy usually did. But for Mickey, it wasn't the easiest thing to do. As he leaned forward to put the jugs on the table, he stumbled. One knee landed on the bench, and he felt the squish of something soft.

"Oh no!" Mom wailed. "My cake!"

Mickey groaned. His knee had settled squarely in the middle of the pan. From beneath the aluminum foil covering, chocolate cake and white frosting oozed onto the bench.

Dad and Troy laughed. Mickey tried to laugh, too, but didn't quite make it. Instead, the hot flush of embarrassment reached his face. When Mom wiped cake off his jeans, Mickey felt like a baby.

Troy would never do such a stupid thing. Mickey wished he could crawl inside a hollow stump.

Soon everyone changed clothes and walked to the beach. For as far as Mickey could see in both directions, sand and water lined the coast. Waves lapped against the shore. Off to the west, the sun edged down toward the water, casting a golden path.

Mom and Dad stretched out on large towels, and Mickey followed Troy into the surf. When he compared his height with Troy's, Mickey felt like a weakling. Just the same, the cold water felt good. Again and again Mickey waded in, dropped on his stomach, and rode the waves back to shore.

While he and Troy swam, the sun dropped lower. As Mickey waded into deeper water, he looked toward the horizon. Blinded by the light, he squinted. It was hard to see Troy, but he was out there again, ahead of Mickey

Knowing that Mom and Dad wanted them to stay together, Mickey struck out toward the sun. But his older brother kept moving farther away.

Mickey felt uneasy. *Troy shouldn't go out that far. Can Mom and Dad see him?*

Half walking, half swimming, he tried to catch up. More than once he called, "Hey, Troy!" When his brother didn't turn, Mickey felt sure that the noise of the surf drowned out his voice.

Now he felt an urgency to catch up to Troy. Were the waves growing larger, or did it just seem that way?

Mickey had almost reached Troy when he cried out. A moment later he disappeared below the surface. When Troy came up again, he frantically waved his arms. Panic filled his voice.

Mickey dived into the waves and swam as fast as he could toward his brother. Soon Mickey couldn't touch bottom. *Did Troy feel the ground fall away? Did a strong current pull him off balance?*

By the time Mickey reached Troy, he was underwater

again. Reaching down, Mickey pulled him up by the hair, then caught Troy's arm.

As Mickey started to pull him toward shore, Troy lashed out. Swinging wildly, he grabbed Mickey around the neck.

Gasping for air, Mickey plunged under the water. As he dragged his brother with him, Troy's grip loosened. Mickey surfaced behind his back, swung an arm around Troy's chest, and started swimming.

Once more Troy struggled, but Mickey's grip held. With a strong arm stroke and powerful kick, he headed toward shore, letting the waves help him.

It seemed forever, but at last Mickey's feet touched bottom. Never before had sand felt so good.

As Mickey helped him stand up, Troy drew a deep breath. The waves washed around him, and he shivered. But Troy spoke through chattering teeth. "Thanks, brother."

Mickey looked in his eyes and knew that something had changed between them. *I don't have to be like Troy,* he thought. *I can just be me.*

TO **TALK** ABOUT

▸ How will it help Mickey to know he doesn't have to be just like Troy? Explain.

▸ How can family position make someone like Mickey feel he isn't worth as much as an older brother or sister?

▸ Do you think Mickey's parents love one boy more than the other? Or do they love each boy for his own special qualities? Give reasons for your answer.

▸ Sometimes it's good to want to be like someone else. It encourages you to live up to their strong qualities. Other times it's *not* good because you don't appreciate the way you are. Which was true in Mickey's case? How do you know?

▸ It took something very big before Mickey realized he had something to offer. You don't have to be a hero like Mickey. **Whoever you are, you have something to offer. You have good qualities that can help you become an in-spite-of-it kid—a kid who isn't stopped by the hard things you face. Your good qualities are gifts from God, and it's important that you know what they are.**

▸ What *good* qualities do *you* have? (Be honest now! It will help your self-esteem.)

▸ Does God play favorites? Or does He love all of us equally, no matter who we are? How do you know?

▸ If you don't have a mom or dad who lets you know they love you for the special person you are, what thought can comfort you?

The Lord will fulfill his purpose for me; your love, O Lord, endures forever. Psalm 138:8

Help me, Lord, to stop comparing my weaknesses with the strengths of others. Thank you that you have given me my own set of strengths and good qualities.

First Day
for Erin

Ready to leave the bedroom she knew so well, Erin looked around. On her bulletin board were reminders of special times—a dried flower from a wedding, a ticket stub from the Milwaukee Zoo, a picture of her friends on the last day of school.

Seeing the picture, Erin felt sad for what was past and afraid of what was ahead. The school district had shut down the small old building where she knew everyone and everything. Her friend Jill would be in the big new school, but most of the other kids were going elsewhere.

Though the day was bright with sunshine, Erin's heart felt cold. As she climbed aboard the school bus, she wondered, *What if I can't remember where my classes are? What if I get lost?*

Sure, there had been a special day for new students. She and Jill and other new kids went through their schedules. But now the school would be full of students who knew each other and had no doubt about where to go.

Butterflies fluttered in Erin's stomach. *What if . . . what if they laugh at me?*

When she reached school, Erin pulled open the heavy

door. The sunshine disappeared in the long halls and endless classrooms.

I can't do it, Erin thought. The words set up a chant in her brain. *I'll never find my way.* Like a spinning bike wheel, the words went round and round in her mind. Then Erin saw Jill.

"Hi, Erin!" Jill called to her. "All set?"

As they met in the hall, Jill's warm smile chased away Erin's scared feelings. *Jill will remember where to go. She always finds her way around.*

Jill chattered as she went. "Good thing we have the same schedule."

Soon she took a right, then a left, then started down another long hall. Confused by all the turns, Erin followed step by step.

I don't remember going this way. She felt glad that her friend took the lead.

"Here it is," Jill said. "Room 111."

The girls slid into seats across from each other. Soon the teacher asked them to open their math books. As Erin looked at the problems, her brain felt fuzzy.

"They're so hard," she whispered to Jill. "You know how dumb I am in math."

When the bell rang, they started out once more. Again Jill took the lead. Turning one way, then another, she climbed a flight of stairs and rounded a corner.

I can't remember this, either. Erin didn't want to admit that she had no idea where they were. *How does Jill manage to do it?*

"Room 238," Jill said as though she had discovered the New World. As far as Erin was concerned, she had.

It was English class. "Just wait," Erin told Jill. "We'll have to write about what we did this summer."

Sure enough. "Do one page," the teacher told them.

"That's easy," Erin said in a low voice. "I did lots of fun things."

But as she bent over her paper, she remembered another class and another time. As though it were yesterday, Erin saw herself in fourth grade, trying to write about her summer. That time she couldn't come up with one sentence. Erin still remembered how she felt when the teacher collected her blank paper.

Now, like a recorder in her head, a tape started to play. *You're going to tell about the time on the beach? That doesn't sound like fun.*

Erin wrote one sentence, then sat back to look at it. *What if this sounds dumb?* she asked herself.

Crumpling up her paper, Erin tried again. Before she knew it, the time was up. Her paper was still blank, but Jill had written two pages.

The bell rang, and Erin followed Jill out of class. One part of Erin wanted to be like Jill. The other part started to resent all the things Jill did well. By this time Erin's fuzzy head felt like splitting. Together they walked down a flight of stairs, around a corner, then into a long hall.

Suddenly Jill stopped in her tracks. "Where are we? You'll have to help me on this one, Erin."

"You really don't know?"

Jill shook her head.

"But all day long you've led us to every class."

Jill giggled. "You think so? You didn't notice I was just going round and round?"

"I thought you knew where you were going," Erin said.

"I didn't know if I could find the rooms. I just kept trying."

Jill grinned. "I figured if I got lost, I could always ask someone—like right now."

In that moment Erin's fuzzy brain cleared. "All day long I thought . . ."

Looking around, Erin recognized a display window. This time she didn't listen to the voice that told her she couldn't do it. "C'mon," she said, wanting to make a new start.

When they found the room they needed, Jill grinned at her. "You know something? You're worth more than you think!"

Jill's words were a happy sound in Erin's ears.

TO **TALK** ABOUT

▸ Erin and Jill faced the same problems, but Erin was afraid of the "what ifs." How did she use those "what ifs" to put herself down? How did that negative habit keep her from doing things?

▸ **The way you look at yourself can become a mountain that keeps you from trying.** You start to believe the negative thoughts you tell yourself. In what ways do you put yourself down?

▸ Are you really a failure in what you've tried to do, or is that something you tell yourself? How do you know?

▸ Erin could tell herself, "If I fail, I can start over again." Why is it better to try and fail than to never try at all?

▸ Your big-time enemy, Satan, wants you to feel you're no good. It's a trick he uses to keep you from becoming all that Jesus wants you to be. Instead of letting enemy thoughts go round and round in your head, let the Holy Spirit help you. The minute an enemy thought enters your mind, choose to think about a Bible verse you know. Repeat that verse until it becomes real to you.

▸ **God's Word has the power to change the way you think.** For some Bible verses that give you courage, check out Deuteronomy 31:8; Joshua 1:9; and Isaiah 41:10, 13.

▸ **In-spite-of-it kids know that Jesus gives the power to do whatever He asks them to do.** How can memorizing Bible verses help you become an in-spite-of-it kid?

I can do everything God asks me to with the help of Christ who gives me the strength and power. Philippians 4:13 (TLB)

Forgive me, Jesus, for telling myself I can't do things even before I try. Help me to stop putting myself down. Help me to find my confidence and strength in you. Thanks that if I trust in you, you will help me reach my best.

Corey Goes to Camp

"Hey, we're here!" Corey poked Nate and pointed to a sign outside the car window. "See? Spirit Point Camp!"

For two months Corey had looked forward to church camp. Now the big moment had come!

Nate leaned across Corey, trying to see. Sure enough, the arrow pointed off to the right. Minutes later they climbed out of the car and said good-bye to Nate's dad. A counselor showed them where to go.

The cabin they entered had one large room with six bunk beds. Two other boys were already there. Suddenly Corey felt shy about meeting them. He was glad he'd been able to come with a friend. Nate would know what to say.

As usual, he helped Corey out. "Hi, I'm Nate," he said to the boys in the cabin. "This is my friend Corey."

A short boy with dark hair popped up from where he was putting away his clothes. "I'm Alfonse, and this is Jay. We're from Waite Park. How about you?"

Soon Nate had stowed his clothes, and he and Alfonse decided to check out the beach. Not sure what to do, Corey followed them and sat down on the dock to listen.

Wish I could act like Nate, he thought. *He always finds something to talk about.*

A moment later Nate and Alfonse headed for the place that sold munchies. There they found more kids. Soon Alfonse introduced Nate to his friends from home. But Corey hung back, afraid to meet them. *I'll never think of something to say,* he told himself.

By suppertime Corey felt lost and alone. When the bell rang for lights-out, he crawled into bed, glad that the day was over. A knot of misery formed in his stomach.

Burying his face in the pillow, Corey let his loneliness sink in. It was a long time before he fell asleep.

When he woke up the next morning, Corey discovered Nate and Alfonse had gone to the early-bird swim. *Now what do I do?* Corey wondered.

Corey looked for Alfonse's friend Jay but couldn't see him. The other guys were all getting dressed. Afraid that everyone would leave him behind, Corey got up and pulled on his jeans.

Soon he was ready, but he pretended he had more to do. The loneliness he felt the night before was growing.

Just then Nate and Alfonse came into the cabin. Picking up a volleyball, Nate threw it to Alfonse. "Catch!" he called, and both boys laughed as though they had a private joke.

I wish I could go home, Corey thought. *I'll never make it through a whole week.*

Everyone in the cabin went to breakfast together, but Corey walked without talking, unable to think of anything to say. At breakfast Nate and Alfonse sat at one end of the table, still laughing over something that had happened while swimming. Corey sat at the other end, staring at his hot cakes. For the first time in his life, he wasn't hungry.

Just then the camp director rang a bell. "Small groups in

ten minutes! Look at your name tag, and it will tell you where to go."

Corey glanced at his tag. Nate's had a different shape, so they'd be separated again. *I wonder if I can sneak back to the cabin and hide,* thought Corey. But soon the kids were getting rid of their dirty dishes. Corey found Jay waiting for him.

"Looks like we're in the same group," he said. "Let's go together."

Minutes later they were part of a circle sitting on the grass outside the dining hall. "I'm Tim," said their leader. "And I know you're from many different churches. Let's start by each of you getting to know one other person. The easiest way is to ask questions. What are some questions you might ask?"

No one spoke. Tim sat there, waiting.

"What's the first thing you want to know about a person?" he asked.

"Their name," answered someone across the circle.

"Good. What else?"

"Where they live."

"Great!" Tim said. "Got any more ideas?"

No one spoke. "Then I've got some questions. Any of you have a giraffe at home?"

Everyone laughed.

"How about an elephant?"

Again they laughed.

"Well, what *do* you have at home?"

"A brother!" yelled someone, as though she didn't like the idea.

Someone else caught on. "A sister!"

"Gerbils!" "Ten goldfish!" "A guinea pig!"

27

"Ahhh!" Tim said. "Now, have you got something you can ask a person besides their name?"

As Corey listened he made a discovery. *All I have to do is figure out what someone else wants to talk about.*

Tim split them up into pairs. Corey felt relieved that he could be with Jay. Now he knew what to say. "I know your name, but do you live in town or on a farm?"

It wasn't long before he discovered Jay had a pony named Patches, two sisters, and one brother. And he wanted to go fishing that afternoon.

Maybe he's been feeling the way I have, thought Corey, grateful that he had a new friend.

Corey settled into a more comfortable position, surprised to discover he no longer felt lonely. The week ahead stretched out before him, filled with promise.

TO **TALK** ABOUT

▸ How did Corey depend on Nate? Is it good to depend on someone that much? Why or why not?

▸ When Corey was lonely, who was he thinking about? How did focusing on himself keep him feeling lonely?

▸ Sometimes kids feel homesick when they're away from home. Do you think that was part of Corey's problem? Why or why not?

▸ When did his loneliness start to disappear? How did Corey become an in-spite-of-it kid who reached out to someone else?

▸ If you want to choose between shyness and making a new friend, what are some questions you can ask?

- How do you think Corey felt about himself after he made friends with Jay? Why do you think that?

- There was someone Corey forgot. Who was that person? How did He help Corey, even though Corey forgot about Him?

- **Jesus wants to be your closest friend. In what ways can you reach out to Him?**

"When you pass through the waters, I will be with you; and when you pass through the rivers, they will not sweep over you." Isaiah 43:2

Thank you, Jesus, that you have promised to be with me. Thank you that you're always my friend. When I'm lonely, help me remember that. Help me go beyond my shyness and reach out to others.

Christmas Love

As the kids at school talked, Joanna wanted to put her hands over her ears. She wished she could shut out the sound of their words. Their voices sounded like hammers pounding on steel.

"Your mom dropped you on a doorstep," said one of the girls.

"She didn't want you," added another.

The minute Joanna could get away, she took off for home. By the time she was out of sight from the kids, she could no longer hold back her tears. As they streamed down her cheeks, Joanna broke into a run. When she reached the front door, she was panting.

Joanna stopped long enough to take a deep breath, then quietly slipped inside. *Maybe I can get to my bedroom without anyone seeing me.*

But the little Christmas bells on the door gave her away. As she tiptoed toward the steps, Mom came into the hall.

"Joanna! What's going on?"

Joanna kept moving, but as she passed under the light, Mom stopped her. "What's the matter?" she asked gently.

Joanna wondered if her cheeks were streaked from crying. "Nothing," she said.

"You can tell me, you know," Mom answered.

"I said *nothing!*" snapped Joanna, the hurt within her
changing to anger. "I mean *nothing!*"

But Mom put an arm around her shoulder. "Dad's home,
and we've been putting up the tree. Come and see."

Knowing there was no escape, Joanna walked slowly into
the family room. The tree was beautiful, the tallest she could
remember. Dad stood on a chair, putting lights on the
branches near the top. When he saw Joanna, he climbed
down to give her a hug.

"Have a hard day?" he asked.

Joanna shrugged. She didn't want to say what was wrong.
But as Dad gave her another hug, the words tumbled out.

"The kids at school said I was adopted."

Joanna saw the look that passed between Mom and Dad,
but it was Dad who spoke first.

"You know that. We've talked about it lots of times. Why
is it bothering you now?"

"One of the kids heard her mom talking about me. She
said my mother didn't want me, and that's why you adopted
me."

Joanna's shoulders began to shake. "She said my mom
dropped me on a doorstep. My own *mother* didn't want me!
I wasn't worth anything, not even to her. I'm just . . . just—"

Joanna broke off and plopped into Dad's big chair. "I'm
just a big zero!" she wailed.

Dad sat down on the floor, cross-legged, in front of her.
Mom pulled up a chair beside her. Joanna's sobs increased.
She needed to know someone loved her. But she didn't know
how to say it or how to ask all the things she wanted to know.

As she blew her nose, Dad spoke. "Joanna, do you remember what we've told you about your birth mother?"

Joanna nodded her head, and Dad went on.

"We know your mother was only sixteen when you were born. And it's true that she left you on a doorstep. But social workers found out who she was. They told us she would have had a very hard time taking care of you. She didn't have any way to give you a good home."

Mom reached forward and gently pushed the hair out of Joanna's eyes. "Do you remember your first doll?"

Joanna nodded.

"Everywhere you went you took that doll. You wanted to hug it and hang on to it. We learned that your mother felt that way about you. She wanted to keep you. It hurt her to give you up."

"You were very special to her," Dad said. "But she let go of her own wishes. She believed someone else would give you a better life."

Joanna searched Dad's face. "But the kids said she didn't *want* to keep me—that she didn't *want* to be my mother."

"She *did* want to. She loved you so much that she wanted to give you a good home. She let you be adopted because she wanted to give you the best opportunity to be happy."

Joanna drew a deep breath. "That's really true?"

"Really true," echoed Dad. "And we wanted you very much. We chose to have you."

"But you didn't know me," answered Joanna. "I was just a little baby. You didn't know what I'd be like."

"We had prayed about you," Dad answered. "We believed that no matter what you'd be like, God wanted you to be part of our family."

Dad grinned. "And we got the best end of the deal!"

Joanna looked into Dad's eyes. Again she searched his face. Something stirred inside her, a warm feeling that Dad really meant what he said.

She thought about it for a moment, letting the warmth of being loved sink in. Then another thought struck Joanna. *I'm thirteen, and my mom was only three years older when she had me.*

The idea of taking care of a baby full time scared Joanna. She wondered if that was how her birth mother felt.

"Joanna, Dad and I love you very much," Mom said. "I think you're forgetting why we gave you your name. Remember what it means?"

"God is gracious," answered Joanna.

"That means God is kind," Mom said. "You're our special gift from Him."

Now Mom had tears in her eyes. "Joanna, we don't know yet how it will affect your life that you lived with us instead of your birth mother. But as you grow up, let God show you good things about it."

As the tears brimmed over onto Mom's cheeks, Joanna crawled out of Dad's chair. This time it was Joanna who gave the hugs.

TO **TALK** ABOUT

▸ To be rejected means to be unwanted. When Joanna thought her birth mother didn't want her, how did she feel about herself?

▸ In what ways did Joanna's adoptive parents show their love? How did they help Joanna know she was special to them?

▸ **Every one of us needs to know we're loved just the way we are.** Do you ever wonder if you're loved? Why is it important to talk to your mom or dad about it? What would you like to say?

▸ Do you know someone who is adopted? How has it changed that person's life?

▸ Were you adopted? What questions do you have that you've never asked your adoptive parent or parents?

▸ There is someone who *always* loves you exactly the way you are. Who is that person?

▸ **No matter what your birth situation was, God the Father saw you before you were born. He is the one who formed and created you. If you don't know how much He loves and cares about you, ask Him to make that real to you.**

When my bones were being formed, carefully put together in my mother's womb, when I was growing there in secret, you knew that I was there—you saw me before I was born. Psalm 139:15–16a (TEV)

Those who trust in the Lord are protected by his constant love. Psalm 32:10b (TEV)

Jesus, I choose to look to you in everything that happens to me. Help me to know down deep how much you love me. Thank you that even before I was born, your Father was my Father and saw and cared about me. Thanks that I'm a valuable person in your sight and in His.

Which Way Back?

"Dillon, you're grounded," Dad said in his I-mean-business voice. "When I ask you to help with dishes, I want you to help. And you don't have to talk back. We're a family. We should be courteous to one another."

Dillon stalked out of the room, anger in every cell of his body.

"Don't forget. Stay in the cabin," Dad called after him.

Soon the cabin was quiet. Lying on his bed in the loft, Dillon heard his sister and brother and Dad and Mom leave for the boat. It wasn't hard to guess what a picnic on the island would be like.

There'd be a heavy basket filled with his favorite food. The mid-August sun would still be warm. As if he were there, Dillon imagined the swimming beach, the sun sparkling on the water, and the feel of sand between his toes. His sister and brother would build huge castles in the sand with large moats around them.

If Dad thinks I'm going to stay inside all afternoon, he's got another guess coming, Dillon told himself. *I've been wanting to explore the woods around here. I'll do it on my own.*

Like a tiny whisper, he seemed to hear Dad's voice. *"You're used to living in the city. Don't go into the woods alone. If two of you want to go together, tell us first. Let us know what direction you're taking and wear your whistles."*

"Phooey!" Dillon answered the inner voice. *I'm not gonna wear a cord with a whistle on it. I'm not a baby. I'll go to the pond we found last summer. And* nothing *will happen to me. I'll get away with it!*

Outside, Dillon found the wind had changed, so he returned to the cabin for a sweat shirt. When he couldn't find his own, Dillon snatched up his brother's and pushed it into his knapsack. Then he took off through the woods.

He found the pond without difficulty. Clear and still, with only an occasional ripple, the water hugged the shore. Nearby, a stronger current passed into another pond, and a great beaver lodge rose from the surface.

Soon Dillon spotted other signs of beavers at work—a large birch with a portion of bark peeled off, and a poplar almost gnawed through. Wood chips surrounded its base. Farther on, Dillon saw an even bigger poplar down. Only a sharp, pointed stump remained.

Excitement filled him. *I'll bring everyone back to see this.*

A moment later Dillon remembered. *Uh-oh! I can't. I'll have to pretend I haven't been here.* The good feeling about his discovery vanished. *Well, I'd better get back before they find out I'm gone.*

Starting off, he followed the pressed-down line of grass he knew to be a deer path. *Looks like an easier way to the cabin,* he thought.

Soon the birch and poplar trees merged into a large pine

woods. Dillon came to the top of a hill and looked down. Row after row of tall pine trees stretched as far as he could see. The lower branches had broken off as the upper ones reached for the sun. Beneath them, fallen needles formed a soft brown carpet.

The wind whispered through the trees as Dillon started between them. Here and there a tall pine creaked, as though a squeaky door swung in the wind.

Dillon began filling his knapsack with cones, then remembered he couldn't take them home. Emptying them out, he started to walk faster and came to the edge of the pines. Down the hill and off to his right a pond nestled in a hollow.

The sun had disappeared under clouds, and the water looked dark and cold. But somehow the pond seemed strangely familiar.

It was. Around the edge were the trees the beavers had gnawed.

The first finger of uneasiness jabbed Dillon's ribs. *I've walked in a circle,* he told himself. *How do I get home?*

The hidden sun offered no clue. Trying to push down his fear, Dillon started to hurry. *They'll get back and find me gone.*

Following the shore, he circled the pond. Stickers clutched at his jeans. Overhanging branches grabbed at his knapsack and shirt. Panic filled him.

Starting to run, Dillon jumped logs and brushed through tall weeds. Suddenly he stepped into a hole and crashed down.

A sharp flash shot through his ankle. "Ow, ow, ow!" he groaned. The whole world seemed to spin. Dizzy with pain, Dillon rolled on the ground.

Finally he pushed his elbows into the soft earth and tried

to sit up. Every movement was agony. The rising wind chilled him.

Dillon shivered. *It's getting darker and cooler all the time. Dad* did *know how big these woods are. What am I going to do?*

Dillon didn't want to admit how scared he felt, but tears of pain and fear pushed against his eyes. *Maybe Dad was right about bringing a whistle.*

For the first time Dillon regretted what he had done. "Forgive me, God," he prayed. "I'm sorry, God. Sorry I didn't do what Dad said."

The scared feeling didn't go away, but at least Dillon felt as if he could think. Dragging himself on his elbows and good leg, he reached the backpack he had dropped. As he pulled out his brother's sweat shirt, Dillon felt a small, hard object.

Frantically he fumbled in the pocket. A moment later he found a long cord. On it, a whistle!

This time Dillon didn't think about what Dad would say because he disobeyed. He just felt glad that his family would care about him. *Are they back at the cabin?* he wondered. *Will they hear me?*

With every breath in his body, he blew a long, shrill whistle.

TO **TALK** ABOUT

▸ Do you think Dillon's family will find him? Why do you think that?

▸ Dillon's problem started with not wanting to do dishes. How did one problem build on top of another?

▸ It's hard to like yourself if there's something wrong in your closest relationships. How did sin separate Dillon from his family? How can sin separate you from God and other people?

▶ If you do something wrong, feel sorry for your sin, and ask God for forgiveness, He *will* forgive you. Because Dillon was sorry and asked forgiveness, God forgave him. But does that mean everything will suddenly be all right? Give reasons for your answer.

▶ **When you make a choice, there will be good or bad consequences.** Something will happen as a result of your choice. If you make a good choice, there are usually good consequences. If you make a bad choice, there are often bad consequences.

▶ What are the *bad* consequences of Dillon's choice to disobey? Can you think of any *good* consequences that might come out of what Dillon did? Why or why not?

▶ What are some *bad* consequences you've experienced because of choices you made? What are some *good* consequences coming out of choices you made?

▶ How do you think Dillon's dad will show his love to Dillon?

The Lord corrects those he loves, as parents correct a child of whom they are proud. Proverbs 3:12 (TEV)

Forgive me, Jesus, when I sin against you and other people. I'm sorry for the wrong things I do. Thank you that when I'm truly sorry, you forgive me and help me change.

Something to Offer

Spring sunlight warmed Heather's face as she leaned against the wall of the school. Yet the warmth of the sun was not in her heart.

She always dreaded this moment. Whenever the girls in her class played softball, Heather relived her fear of being chosen last.

As she watched, Marita and Kim took their places. *Why do they always get to be captains?* Heather asked herself. Of course she knew. They were the best players. Yet she felt upset over something that never seemed to change.

Soon the choosing of sides began. "Caitlin!" called out Marita.

"Brianna!" shouted Kim.

And so it went. One moment Heather pressed hard against the wall, wishing she could disappear forever. The next she stood as tall as possible, hoping Marita or Kim would notice her.

If I could at least be somewhere in the middle, thought Heather. *I can't stand it if I'm last again.*

But she was. When no one else was left, Marita called her

name. Full of misery, Heather went forward, hating even the ground she had to cross.

I'll show 'em, she thought. *I'll play so well that next time they'll* want *me on their team.*

Trying to walk as if she knew what she was doing, Heather hurried to her usual place in right field. For a long time nothing happened. Heather stood there, kicking blades of grass and squinting against the sun. Then a long, slow fly ball headed her way.

Heather ran forward. *If only I can—* She reached for it. The ball hit her mitt and dropped to the ground.

Grabbing wildly, Heather stumbled and fell on the ball. As she scrambled up, two runners crossed home plate. Desperately she threw the ball to second, but she was too late. Moments later the runner touched third.

"Way to go, butterfingers!" someone called.

Heather's face felt as if it had caught fire. The rest of the afternoon it burned. When she returned to school the next morning, Heather still felt the flames of embarrassment.

She was glad when Mr. Lopez asked them to take out their math books. Heather flew through the problems. As she finished, she looked up. Everyone else was still working.

Across the aisle, Marita was doodling with a pencil. Today she didn't seem like a softball captain. One look told Heather that Marita was as confused as ever.

Secretly Heather felt glad. *Nice to know I can beat her at something!*

But a moment later Marita looked her way. "Can you help me, Heather?" she whispered. "My head feels like it's spinning."

Forget it! Heather nearly spit out. *When you always choose me last? I should help* you?

In the next instant, Heather felt ashamed of her thoughts. Raising her hand, she got permission from Mr. Lopez, then slid her desk closer to Marita's.

"I just don't get it at all," Marita said in a low voice.

Step by slow step, Heather started to explain. Each time she saw a confused look in Marita's face, Heather backed up a bit, then worked forward again.

At last a light seemed to turn on behind Marita's eyes. "Wow, Heather! How do you do it? You help me so much!"

In that moment Mr. Lopez asked for their attention. "I just received a note from the office about why Kim isn't in school today. It's really bad news. Her house caught fire last night. By the time the firemen got there, it had burned to the ground."

"Oh no!" The gasp went through the room. Heather saw the shock in the faces around her.

"All of Kim's family got out safely," Mr. Lopez went on. "But they have nothing left but the clothes they were wearing."

Again Heather looked around the classroom. She wondered if her face looked as scared as everyone else's. *How awful! What if someone* hadn't *gotten out?*

Then Heather remembered how she had felt about Kim being one of the captains. Somehow being chosen last didn't matter anymore. Instead, Heather felt relieved that Kim was okay.

Her thoughts leaped ahead. *What would it be like to have nothing at all?*

"Let's think of what we can do to help Kim and her family," said Mr. Lopez.

For a moment everyone was quiet. In the stillness Heather seemed to be playing softball again. All her feelings of helplessness returned. *What can I do? It seems I can't do any-thing right.*

Then Marita waved her hand. "I'm the same size as Kim," she blurted out. "I'll bring some of my clothes."

Paul chimed in. "I have little brothers the same age as Kim's brothers. I'll ask my mom for some of their things."

"We can bring cans of food," another girl said. "Do they have a place to stay?"

Heather was still thinking. Her mind seemed frozen by yesterday and how stupid she felt. Again she wondered, *Is there really any way I can help?*

As though hearing her question, Paul spoke again. "Maybe we should bring money."

"Good idea," said Mr. Lopez. "They'll need to buy a lot of things."

In that instant a thought flashed through Heather's mind. *I can't play softball, but I sure know how to add money.*

Her hand went up. "If you want, I'll collect the money and turn it in to Mr. Lopez."

The teacher nodded, looking grateful.

Heather leaned back in her desk. For the first time since yesterday, she felt peaceful inside, as though she had a place. She had something to offer.

TO **TALK** ABOUT

▸ Heather made a choice to help both Marita and Kim. Why was that hard for her to do? What negative feelings did she have to put aside?

▸ Heather promised to collect the money. What do you think she will gain as she helps someone else? When you've helped others, how have you felt about yourself?

▸ The next time the girls play softball, Marita could choose Heather sooner, even though Heather doesn't play well. But how could Marita help Heather improve her game?

▸ Are there ways in which you feel you can't succeed? What are they? Could you improve if someone helped you? Why is it important to grow in your skills if possible? Think of someone you can ask to help you grow.

▸ **When you aren't able to succeed at something, you can *compensate*, or make up for what you can't do, by achieving in other ways.** In what ways did Heather compensate for her clumsiness in softball? Can you think of ways you've learned to compensate for skills you don't have?

▸ When Jesus was here on earth, He helped His disciples become in-spite-of-it people by showing them how to help others in practical ways. What did Jesus do? For clues see John 13:1–5.

[Jesus said,] "Give to others, and God will give to you. Indeed, you will receive a full measure, a generous helping, poured into your hands—all that you can hold. The measure you use for others is the one that God will use for you." Luke 6:38 (TEV)

Jesus, it bothers me when I can't do things I really want to do. If you want me to learn, give me someone who will help me. Or show me the things I can do well and help me grow in those areas. Thank you!

After the Play

The high school play needed some younger boys, and D.J. and three of his friends were chosen. Being in the cast was the most fun he'd had in a long time.

Now the curtain fell on their last performance, then swept open again. Together the cast ran onto the stage. As they took their final bows, the applause grew. Here and there people rose from their seats. Others joined in a standing ovation.

Wow! thought D.J. *They really liked it. Guess it was worth all the work!*

As the curtain closed around them, his classmate Tad found him in the crowd. "Hey, D.J., we're having a party."

"You mean with the juniors and seniors?"

"Nah, our own party. I asked a bunch of kids, and they're asking their friends. We'll meet at my house. Have your mom and dad drop you off."

D.J. felt torn. One part of him thought, *I want to go. It should be fun.* The other part wondered, *What kind of a party will it be?*

He knew why they'd go to Tad's. His parents hadn't come to the play, and they wouldn't be at home, either. They were always out somewhere.

The thought made D.J. uncomfortable, but he still wanted to go. *Maybe I can witness to them about Jesus,* he told himself.

Forty-five minutes later, D.J. and his friend Carlos stood on Tad's front step. Through the closed door and windows, the beat of a strong bass rose and fell. D.J. pounded on the door. When no one heard them, he and Carlos walked in.

Tad met them on the stairs to the basement. "Hey, guys! Glad you could make it. There's food on the bar."

"All ri-i-ight!" D.J. was hungry. He took the steps in a bound and found the room full of kids.

"Hi, D.J.!" called out one kid after another. "Good show!" said many. "You were great!" By the time he reached the bar, D.J. felt warmed by their praise.

With the music thumping around him, he heaped his plate with food. *What a night!* he thought as he saw all the good munchies. *First the play, now this.*

A moment later D.J. crashed to earth. Tad entered the room with two six-packs of beer in his hands.

Someone turned down the music. Tad stood on a chair, holding high a can of beer. "Let's give a toast for the best play this side of Chicago!"

A cheer went up. Another boy grabbed a can, raising it above his head. "And let's give a toast to the best girls in the state!"

Setting down his food, D.J. glanced at Carlos. Carlos looked just as uncomfortable as D.J. felt.

D.J. worked his way over to Tad. "Hey, where'd you get the beer?"

"My older brother bought it for us. What's it to you?"

"You know we're breaking the law."

"So? Big deal."

"What if our parents or the cops find out? We'll be in big trouble."

"Who's gonna give us away? You and Carlos are the only guys who might squeal."

D.J. looked around and knew Tad was right. Then another idea struck him. "What if a neighbor complains about the noise?"

"They never do," Tad answered. "Forget it."

In that moment D.J. knew he'd been fooling only one person. *Be a witness here?* he asked himself. *Who am I trying to kid?*

Tad began throwing beer cans to the kids around the room. Someone cranked up the CD player again.

D.J. edged over to Carlos. "I don't like this. Let's get out of here."

The music beating around him, D.J. bounded up the steps and out the front door. Carlos followed him.

Once outside, D.J. breathed deep. "Want some burgers?" he asked Carlos. Together they headed off down the street.

As they reached the corner a block away, D.J. saw a squad car turn into the block. Turning around to watch, D.J. saw the policemen pull into the driveway of Tad's house.

TO **TALK** ABOUT

▸ Who do you think called the police? Why? What do you think happened to the kids at the party? What do you think happened to Tad's brother for buying the beer?

▸ Do you believe D.J. *really* thought he would witness for Jesus at the party? Why or why not?

▸ If you were D.J. or one of the girls at the party, how would you feel about being there? Do you feel awkward about being in some places? Why or why not?

▸ How is that a different kind of awkwardness than what Corey felt when he was new at camp ("Corey Goes to Camp," p. 25)?

▸ **Not feeling at home in every crowd can be your protection. Sometimes you may feel uneasy because you *know* something isn't right. Or the Holy Spirit might warn you about something you can't actually see.** For instance, kids might put something alcoholic into punch at a party. If you feel uneasy about something, pray with your eyes open. Ask Jesus to show you what you need to know.

▸ Knowing what to do when you feel uneasy gives you an escape route. By leaving the party, D.J. made a choice and avoided a lot of difficult consequences. What are some choices you can make if you feel uneasy about what's going on? Explain. Why is it important to know when it's time to leave a place?

▸ **Kids who have self-esteem based on what God thinks about them are able to do what's right in spite of what other kids think.** Have there been times when you went along with what kids were doing and felt sorry later? Have there been other times when you *didn't* go along with what other kids planned? What happened? How did you feel about yourself afterward?

▸ If it wasn't safe or it was too far for D.J. and Carlos to walk home, what else could they have done? Do you and your parents have an agreement that you can call them at any time of the day or night if you need a ride or some other kind of help? How can you work that out in a practical way?

▶ When you hurt because of what kids think about your choices to do right, what helps you feel better? **Whose opinion of you matters the most?**

▶ How did people make fun of Jesus because of the way He chose to live? Why did He want to live as He did?

Flee the evil desires of youth, and pursue righteousness, faith, love and peace, along with those who call on the Lord out of a pure heart. 2 Timothy 2:22

Jesus, when I get mixed up in something wrong, I'm afraid to do the right thing. Show me what to do, then give me your Holy Spirit's power to do it. Help me to think and look ahead so I don't get mixed up in something wrong again. Thank you, Jesus!

You're My Friend, Kate

Kate looked down at her skirt. No matter which way she twisted it, she just couldn't make it fit right. Even worse, the material was starting to fade from the many times it had been washed.

Hastily she stuffed her shorts and shoes into her book bag. Up till this year, she had liked gym the best of any class. Now she was starting to hate this moment. It always made her realize the difference between her clothes and those of the other girls.

Across the locker room, her friend Libby stood in front of a mirror. As Kate watched, Libby carefully brushed her long hair until it hung smoothly down her back. But it wasn't Libby's silky auburn hair that made Kate feel out of it. It was her new designer jeans.

Libby turned, saw Kate watching, and grinned. "Ready to go?"

Kate nodded. Weaving their way through the crowded halls, they reached the great outdoors and started for home. Because they lived only two houses apart, they had known each other for years.

The spring sunshine reminded Kate of a time long ago. Suddenly she laughed.

"What's funny?" Libby asked.

"Do you remember the day I met you?"

Libby's smile lit her face. "How could I forget? I had set up a stand in front of our house, and I was selling . . ."

"Mud pies!" they shouted together, laughing at the memory.

"I ran home and got a penny," said Kate.

"So you could buy one!" Libby finished.

"And you were smeared from head to toe with mud. It had even dried on your face."

Again Libby laughed. "But I was in business!"

Kate joined in her laughter, then was quiet. They'd been together so long that now and then she took Libby for granted. Though they'd been best friends for years, something was changing.

Libby broke the silence. "Kate, is something wrong?"

Kate shook her head. She didn't want to admit how she felt.

"Are you sure?"

"Yup, I'm sure," Kate said.

"You'd tell me if something was wrong?"

Kate started kicking a stone along the edge of the street. *I'd like to bring back the old days,* she thought. *Sometimes I feel so far away from Libby.* Yet she felt embarrassed to say anything.

"Remember how we always shared secrets?" asked Libby. "Even when I made only one penny on mud pies?"

Kate smiled, but the ache didn't leave her heart. *I'm afraid to tell her,* she thought. *Maybe she won't like me anymore.*

But Libby knew her too well. "Spit it out, Kate," she said.

Kate debated with herself, trying to decide what to do. At last she spoke. "You know how my dad got laid off a year ago?"

Libby nodded.

"He still hasn't found work. Mom and Dad don't say much, but they seem different—worried, I guess. Last week I asked if we'll be able to stay here. Dad said, 'We'll keep trying with what your mother makes.' "

"Oh, Kate, I'm so glad! I don't know what I'd do if you moved."

Libby's words gave Kate courage. In spite of the lump in her throat, she went on. "But sometimes I don't feel like your friend anymore. We used to be alike, and now we're different."

"Different?"

When Kate didn't answer, Libby asked, "What do you mean?"

Kate could barely get the words out. "Our clothes," she said.

"Ohhh." Understanding came into Libby's eyes. "And that's why you've been acting funny lately?"

Kate nodded.

"But clothes shouldn't make any difference between us!"

Afraid that Libby would see how she felt, Kate looked off at the house they were passing. "Doesn't it bother you to walk down the hall with me? To have kids see the way I look? My clothes are so old. . . ."

Kate choked on the words, hardly able to speak. "And you have new designer jeans."

Libby stopped right where she was. Kate had to stop, too. "Is that all that's bothering you?"

Kate blinked, trying to hide her tears. "I don't look like

the other kids. There's no money for clothes."

For a long moment Libby was silent. When she spoke, she sounded as if she'd been thinking hard. "Kate, what if you had designer jeans and I didn't? How would you treat me?"

The question surprised Kate. Her gaze met Libby's. "It wouldn't make any difference."

Libby laughed. "What did you say?"

"That it wouldn't make any difference." Kate stopped, suddenly feeling foolish.

For a moment they walked on without speaking. Then Libby broke the silence. "I've got an idea," she said.

Kate looked at her and waited, afraid to hope.

TO **TALK** ABOUT

▶ Both Libby and Kate discovered something important about clothes. What did Libby have to know how to handle? What did Kate?

▶ Libby showed she was a true friend by asking Kate what was wrong. What would have happened if Kate hadn't told her?

▶ How did Libby help Kate believe her worth as a person didn't depend on clothes?

▶ What idea do you think Libby had? How do you suppose she helped Kate with her problem?

▶ Why does it seem important to dress the way other kids do? Have there been times when you've felt embarrassed because your clothes weren't the same? What did you do about it?

▶ What if you were concerned about something and a friend

didn't ask what was bothering you, or try to help? What could you do to start talking?

▶ What did Jesus tell us about the clothes that we wear? See Matthew 6:25–33 for clues. **In what way does Jesus want us to keep our eyes on Him?** If needed, take another look at the verses in Matthew.

"For the Lord does not see as man sees; for man looks at the outward appearance, but the Lord looks at the heart." 1 Samuel 16:7b (NKJV)

Help me, Lord, to look my best with what I have. But protect me from thinking I'm worth something only if I have the right clothes. I want to please you with the way I am in my heart.

Angelo Carries the Pigskin

Angelo gripped the football, lifted it behind his ear, and took one step ahead. With a snap of the wrist, he sent a long pass to Dad.

"Great!" Dad called out with approval. "Now let me show you a trick play."

Angelo liked playing football with Dad. He knew it gave him an advantage over many of the boys. Yet sometimes . . .

Dad moved closer. "You can teach this to Justin and do it together. You grip the ball and hold it behind your head as if you're going to pass. Like this, see?"

Angelo watched.

"As I hold the ball, you run up behind and take it."

Angelo moved out. Running hard, he grabbed the ball from Dad's hands and kept going.

"Now try it the other way," said Dad. "Pretend you're going to pass. I'll take it off you."

With split-second timing, Angelo lifted the pigskin. Dad grabbed it and kept going.

"Way to go!" Dad shouted.

His praise warmed Angelo. He knew he was getting better

all the time. He also knew he had the build to become a good player. If only . . .

Dad slapped him across the shoulders. "You're just a chip off the old block."

That's what bothers me, thought Angelo. *What if I can't do as well as Dad did?*

"You'll be just as good a player as I was—better, in fact!" Dad said as though reading Angelo's thoughts. "If I hadn't hurt my knee, I'd have made it to the big time."

There it is again, thought Angelo. *He wants me to make it there. What if I'm not good enough?*

That afternoon the question stayed with Angelo during the ride to the football field. Like a long-ago dream, he remembered how he used to look forward to playing football. Somehow it wasn't fun anymore. He wondered if the Lions would be too much for them.

As he walked onto the field, Angelo offered his usual prayer. He asked God to help him play a good and fair game. But today he felt so much pressure that he added a request. *So Dad likes how I play, God.*

At half time Angelo's team, the Bears, was one point behind the Lions. With minutes left to play, Angelo glanced at the sidelines and saw Dad's tense face.

In the huddle Angelo told Justin and the coach about the trick play.

The coach nodded. "It's a good one. I've used it. Let's try it on the next play and see if we can recover. Angelo, take left back. Pick up the ball from Justin and try for the right end. They've got a weak man there."

The whistle blew. Both teams fell into line. Above the cheering crowd, Angelo picked out Dad's voice. "Go for it, Angelo!" He wished Dad wouldn't shout louder than the rest.

As Angelo watched, Justin took his position as quarterback. Muscles tense, Angelo crouched.

The ball snapped into Justin's hands. Gripping the pigskin, he faded back. Holding it up behind his head, he looked as though he were going to pass. In that instant Angelo moved forward, grabbed the ball, and started around the right end.

He'd almost made it when he sensed someone coming up from his left. Twisting, he zigzagged. Knees high, he cleared the other team, running fast.

The crowd roared. *Twenty yards to go,* he thought, the pressure mounting within him.

Just then he heard Dad's voice. "He's coming up, Angelo! Pour it on!"

Angelo turned his head and stumbled. In that instant he lost his timing. A second later he crashed to the ground. The ball popped out of his hands.

Rolling over, Angelo tried to recover, but a Lion tackle landed on the ball. Three minutes later the final whistle blew. The Bears had lost.

Angelo felt sick inside. *I would have made it. If I hadn't heard Dad and turned, I would have made it.*

Shoulders slumped, he climbed into the car, dreading the ride home. He didn't need to look at Dad. Angelo knew he'd be upset.

"You had it in the bag, Angelo. What was the matter with you?" Dad asked.

Angelo picked out a spot on the dashboard and stared straight ahead.

"You know better than to look around. I've told you a hundred times!"

Still Angelo didn't answer, but his anger felt like a river rushing toward a dam. *I just can't be Dad,* he thought. *And*

I can't tell him how I feel. It'd be easier to quit playing football.

The car stopped, and Angelo got out. All he could think about was how much fun it used to be to play with Justin.

TO **TALK** ABOUT

▸ How did Angelo feel about losing the game? Why is it important that he lets his dad know how he feels? What do you think Angelo should tell his dad?

▸ What could Dad say to Angelo to help him become an in-spite-of-it kid? How can he help Angelo enjoy football again?

▸ If Angelo keeps playing but doesn't tell his dad what's wrong, how will it affect his life? How will it affect his relationship with his dad?

▸ Angelo's dad helped him learn important football skills. What's the difference between a parent helping a son or daughter learn important skills and wanting them to live out their own dream? At what point did Angelo start feeling pushed?

▸ At school or at home, is there some way you feel pushed beyond what you can do? If so, talk about it with someone who understands. How is that pushed feeling different from when you yourself want to learn how to do something?

▸ Are there times when you *do* need to stretch in order to learn something, such as math or reading? Explain your answer. How can you get help?

▸ **When Jesus wants us to learn something, He takes**

us step by step to prepare us for bigger and more responsible things. If we learn what He wants us to learn at the right time, we're ready to go on. It becomes fun to grow in doing more difficult things.

▸ What do you believe Jesus wants you to learn right now?

I run in the path of your commands, for you have set my heart free. Psalm 119:32

Help me, Jesus, to learn what you want me to learn but to talk about the things I can't handle. Thank you that I'm valuable to you just the way I am.

How Can I Like *Me*?

Paula slid onto a chair, propped her elbows on the table, and leaned forward to close her mouth around a straw. For several moments she stared down, thinking only about her chocolate malt.

When she picked up her spoon, Paula glanced across the table at Cindy. There she sat, nice and thin. *Just the perfect weight,* thought Paula. *Why do I always look so fat?*

"Watch it!" whispered Cindy. "Big trouble! The guys from school."

Again Paula bent her head over her malt. This time she pretended that she didn't see the two boys coming into the ice cream store. As they headed in her direction, Paula's heart fell to the floor and rolled over.

Passing too close, the larger boy bumped into her chair. "Sorry, Chubs," he said in a loud voice.

Paula stared at her malt, trying not to let the hurt show in her face.

The boys circled the table. When the second boy bumped her chair, he exclaimed, "Uh-oh, so-o-o sorry!"

Without looking at either boy, Paula stood up and started for the door.

The boys followed. "Running away? Scared of us?"

Her eyes flashing anger, Paula faced them. "I'm not scared of you. I can't *stand* you!"

At the cash register she threw down her money. As she headed out the door, she wanted only one thing—a place to hide. A place away from the boys, away from staring eyes, away from her own self.

The minute she reached home, Paula went to the kitchen. *I can't stand those boys!* she told herself. Most of all she couldn't stand their terrible words.

She looked down at her faded jeans—big across the legs, big across the hips. *No matter how big my clothes are, they don't hide how much I weigh.*

Pulling out her baggy sweat shirt, she sighed. *I* want *to be the right weight. I* want *to look good.*

One by one, she opened the cupboard doors, then slammed them shut. After a search, she found the butterballs her mom had hidden. As Paula dropped into a chair, she gulped down a cookie. Soon she reached for another, then still another.

Finally Paula put the cover back on the cookies. *I can't stand those boys,* she thought again. *But most of all, I can't stand myself.*

Paula pushed the cookies back into the farthest corner of the cupboard. Even so, she knew she'd find them again.

Why do I do this? she asked herself. *Every time something goes wrong, I gobble every sweet thing I find.*

This time Paula's upset feelings took the form of a prayer. *Lord, I want to start liking myself. I want to change my old eating habits. Will you help me?*

TO **TALK** ABOUT

▸ Sometimes there's a medical reason why people are over-weight, and we need to be understanding about that. Other times, excess weight comes from poor eating habits. Which do you think is true in Paula's case? Why do you believe that?

▸ **Nearly all of us have something about our bodies that we don't like. We have two choices—to accept the way we are or to make a change.** Is Paula's weight something she needs to accept or something she needs to change? How do you know?

▸ As awful as teasing is, it might tell us something we need to know. An in-spite-of-it kid turns what he or she has learned into something good. How did Paula begin doing that? What people can help her learn better ways to eat?

▸ The Holy Spirit can give Paula greater willpower and help her change her eating habits. But even though Paula asks for God's help, what choice does she need to keep on making?

▸ In her preteen years a girl often goes through a stage where she needs larger-size clothes. Then in a short period of time she grows taller and thins out. What happens to a girl's self-esteem if she doesn't understand this may happen during her growing years?

▸ Sometimes girls think they need to have the tall, slender shape of a professional model. How can it harm a person's health to insist on being too thin?

▸ Is there something you don't like about your own body? Is it something you need to change? If you, like Paula, need new eating habits, what is a practical way to begin? If you ask the people around you, God can use them to help you make new eating choices.

But the fruit of the Spirit is love, joy, peace, patience, kindness, goodness, faithfulness, gentleness and self-control.
Galatians 5:23–24a

Jesus, you love me so much that I know you want me to love myself in a healthy way. In your name I ask for all the power of your Holy Spirit to change my bad eating habits and eat the right foods in the right amounts. I need your self-control to say yes or no about what I take in. In faith I thank you for your help.

70

Mess in the Garage

A wave of hopelessness swept over Jesse as he looked around the garage. Someone had left the door open, and a neighborhood dog got in. Before being discovered, he'd tipped over two garbage cans and emptied them on the floor.

A large mound of firewood cluttered the other side of the garage. Rakes and shovels leaned every which way. Dad's workbench looked as if it had been struck by a tornado.

"Do we have to clean all of it?" Jesse asked.

Mom nodded. "A lot of it is stuff you and Neal haven't put away. I want you to work together."

Jesse groaned. *Spend my whole Saturday this way?*

But Mom went on. "Dad's really tired. He doesn't have enough help at the office right now. He'll work all day just trying to catch up."

Jesse's older brother, Neal, stood there with them. If he felt as overwhelmed by the mess as Jesse did, Neal didn't say anything.

Mom turned to him. "I'll be at church until about one, fixing food for a funeral. When I come back, I want to see this done."

Again it was Jesse who spoke up. "I don't know what to do with all this junk."

"Take one thing at a time. Dad threw the wood inside so it wouldn't get rained on. Stack it along that wall," she said, pointing to a far corner. "If you work together, you'll be surprised how quickly you're done."

She blew them both a kiss and headed for the car.

Jesse started with the firewood. *Stupid old stuff!* he thought. It was hard to remember how much he liked to lie in front of the fire in winter. On this sunny October day, he wanted to be out on his in-line skates.

All the wood was split and ready to stack. With a *thump! bang!* Jesse threw it against the wall. But it wasn't long before he knew that throwing the wood wasn't going to work.

When one side of the stack tumbled down, Jesse turned the logs on the end a different direction. With that end braced, the other end held firmly against the wall. Then Jesse restacked the fallen pieces.

Standing back to see what he'd done, he felt good. The pile looked solid and straight. When Dad came home after working all day, he'd be pleased.

But the garage seemed awfully quiet. Jesse looked around. *Where's Neal?*

Jesse went to a window of the house and yelled to him.

"I'm getting a broom!" Neal shouted back.

Jesse returned to the garage. Taking a stepladder, he pounded long nails into the wall and hung up the shovels and rakes. But when he finished, Neal still wasn't there.

Once again Jesse went to the window and called.

"I'm still looking for the broom!" Neal yelled back.

Jesse sat down on a stump outside the garage. He was angry now. *I'm not gonna work if my brother doesn't!* For a time Jesse sat there, wishing he could take off on his skates.

Finally he decided he didn't want to waste the whole day. *I'll get my half done, and Neal can finish the rest.*

Back in the garage again, Jesse started on Dad's workbench. Before long he had all the tools put away, each on its own peg. Again Jesse felt good inside. But as he looked around, he knew he'd done more than half the work. Where was Neal anyway?

Without making a sound, Jesse crept into the house. There was Neal, lying on the floor, watching a video!

Seeing Jesse, Neal jumped up. "I just found the broom."

"Sure!" Jesse said. "And I just did most of the work!"

"Well, good!" his brother answered. "So we're all done?"

Jesse wanted to belt him one, but Neal was bigger. "I'm sure not gonna do any more. All that's left are the two garbage cans and sweeping the floor. If you don't do it, I'll tell Mom."

"What are you, a mama's boy?" Neal answered.

Jesse caught up the broom and went after Neal. But Neal pulled it from him and strolled out to the garage.

So mad he wanted to throw something, Jesse grabbed an apple and chomped on it furiously. Then he headed back to the garage.

Neal had picked up the stuff from the two garbage cans and started sweeping the floor. Seeing Jesse, Neal waved the broom and smirked.

As Jesse sat down to put on his skates, Mom drove up.

"I'm impressed!" she said, seeing the garage and Neal sweeping the floor. "It's great the way you put everything away, Neal. You really did a nice job. I'm proud of you."

Then she looked at Jesse, ready to leave. "Where are you going, young man? The work isn't done."

"Hey, Mom," Jesse began. "I—"

"Yeah, Jesse, come here," Neal broke in. "Finish sweeping the floor."

"Aw, Mom!" Jesse tried again. "I already did more than half!"

Before Jesse could explain, Neal jumped in again. "Hey, little brother. Don't start making up stories!"

Mom looked from one to the other.

Something inside Jesse crumpled. "Believe me, Mom," he pleaded. All that work and . . .

"You liar!" Neal told Jesse.

Again Mom looked from one to the other. "Stop it, both of you! I've had a hard day with the funeral and all. I can't handle your fighting right now. Just finish this up, okay?"

Slowly she walked to the house. Without speaking, Jesse watched her go. Then he looked around the garage. In the corner the wood was neatly stacked. The workbench was clear and ready for Dad to use. Along the wall hung the rakes and shovels. But Neal would get the credit.

Inside, Jesse didn't feel good anymore. In fact, he felt angry from head to toe.

Slowly he stood up. Just then he remembered how tired Dad had looked as he hurried off to work that morning. Suddenly there was something Jesse knew. What was more important? Getting credit? Or helping Dad?

Okay, I'll give it five more minutes, Jesse promised himself. Before long, he skated off.

TO **TALK** ABOUT

▸ When his mom feels ready to talk again, what do you think Jesse should say to her?

▸ If Jesse has been a good worker before, she'll probably believe his story. If he hasn't been a good worker, she might not. What do you think will happen?

▸ Have you ever worked hard to do something and not gotten credit for it? How did you feel? How did it hurt your self-esteem?

▸ If Jesse talks with his mom and still doesn't get credit for doing most of the work, he could stay angry and spend the rest of his life saying, "It wasn't fair." Some things in life *aren't* fair. But there's something else Jesse can choose to remember. What do you think that might be?

▸ **Over a period of time, the experiences of a family often balance out.** If you remember a time when you felt you were treated unfairly, was there another time when you got the better end of the deal?

▸ Was Jesus always treated fairly? Why or why not?

▸ Jesse's story could have another ending:

Okay, I'll give it five more minutes, Jesse promised himself. Before long, he put on his skates and started off.

Just then Mom called to him. "Jesse!" She hurried outside after him.

"Your brother had a change of heart," she said. "He told me what really happened. Thanks for sticking with the job even when it was hard."

When Mom's arms went around Jesse, he felt like crying. But he would *never* do that.

▸ Why do you like this ending better? What ideas does it give you for how you want to treat members of your family?

"You have been faithful with a few things; I will put you in charge of many things." Matthew 25:21b

Jesus, I hurt inside when someone else gets the credit for something I did well. Please help me explain when I should. Help me sort out my feelings. Thank you that you see everything I do. Thanks that you know and care about my doing things well.

I'd Rather Do It Myself!

When they began to sing, Rosa leaned forward to watch the excitement on Kirsten's face.

"Happy birthday to you. Happy birthday to you. Happy birthday, dear Kirsten . . ."

For a moment Kirsten waited, deciding about her wish. Then with a mighty *whooooff* she blew out every candle.

The girls clapped. "You got your wish!" someone said.

The party with girls from the neighborhood had been fun. As Kirsten's mom cut the cake, Rosa looked around the table. Several girls were laughing. One was ready to pop a balloon. Close by, Rosa saw the heads of two girls reflected in a mirror. One of them was April, the girl sitting next to her.

As Rosa watched, April leaned forward. Turning this way and that, April studied her face in the mirror. Then her hand went up, rubbing the new zits on her nose.

April glanced around the table at each girl. It wasn't hard for Rosa to figure out what April was thinking. *She's worried about her zits. She's wondering if anyone can possibly like her with a few pimples on her nose.*

Deep inside, Rosa sighed. Though she made no sound, it

felt like the wind rustling the autumn leaves. *I wish I had April's problems.*

Restless now, Rosa wished the party would end. Just then April stretched out her legs under the table. When she bumped the brace on her leg, Rosa jumped.

Turning, April apologized. "I'm sorry. Did I hurt you?"

Rosa smiled. "I'm okay. Don't worry about it." She moved her leg, then bent down and pushed her crutches farther beneath her chair.

Soon the party was over, and all the girls crowded into Kirsten's room to pick up their coats. Once again Rosa caught April looking in a mirror as though thinking, *What can I do? How can I hide my zits?*

Leaning her crutches against the wall, Rosa shrugged into her coat. As she thanked Kirsten's mom, she saw that everyone was already ahead of her. *Always the last,* thought Rosa. *It always takes me longer.*

After stuffing her belongings into a book bag, Rosa picked up her crutches again. As the outside door closed behind her, Rosa saw the other girls set out.

They'll have fun walking home, Rosa thought. *And I'll walk alone again.*

In the next minute, Rosa realized that the dropping temperature had changed the light rain to sleet—a sleet so fine that not even Kirsten's mom had noticed it. A thin layer of ice coated the sidewalk.

Ahead of Rosa one of the girls took a flying run. "Wheeee! Race you!" she called out.

When April followed in a long slide, Rosa wished she could do the same. She dreaded the short walk home. Though she lived only a short distance away, the ice would make the trip seem like miles.

For a moment Rosa thought of turning back to ask Kirsten's mom for help. But in the next instant she pushed the idea away. Not for anything would she ask for help.

I can make it, she promised herself. *I'll make it just like any other kid.*

Standing on the wide top step, Rosa set her crutches on the narrow step below. As she swung forward, one of her crutches slid.

Rosa gasped. In the next instant, she landed hard on the cement. Her crutch clattered to the sidewalk below.

April whirled around. With a long slide, she was by Rosa's side. "Here, let me help you," she said.

Rosa shook her head. "I'm okay," she answered quickly. But her whole body felt the jolt. Panic tightened her muscles. *How will I make it home?*

"The sidewalk is icy, too." April gave Rosa a hand up, then offered the crutch.

By now April's friends had stopped. "Hey, hurry up!" they called.

Instead, April slid her hand under Rosa's arm. As Rosa once more started down the steps, April's grip tightened.

When they reached the sidewalk, Rosa still felt afraid. Here, too, her crutches slid on the ice.

"I'll walk home with you," April said quickly.

But Rosa told her, "Thanks, but I live the opposite way from you. I'll be okay."

As if wondering what to do, April glanced toward her friends.

"Go ahead," Rosa said. "They're waiting for you."

Instead, April waved toward the other kids. "Go on without me!" she called.

Then April turned back to Rosa. "Just tell me what to do.

I've often wanted to help you but didn't know how."

Startled, Rosa's words spilled out. "You didn't know?"

April shook her head. "You always seem so independent. Like you don't need anyone's help."

Like I don't want *anyone's help,* Rosa thought.

But now April asked, "Would it be easier walking on the grass? It wouldn't be so slippery."

As they set out together, Rosa's thoughts ran ahead. *Maybe I try too hard. Maybe I push kids away. I wonder if they're afraid to be friends?*

By the time she and April reached Rosa's house, they were laughing and talking together. Rosa had also noticed something. *April forgot about her zits.*

Just thinking about it, Rosa felt glad. *Maybe I helped* her *today. Maybe I have a new friend.*

TO **TALK** ABOUT

▸ What do you think was worse—April's zits or how she felt about them? How do you know?

▸ What did Rosa mean when she thought, *I wish I had her problems*? How did April choose to forget about herself?

▸ Instead of trying to walk home, Rosa could have gone back inside to ask for help. Why did Rosa want to make it on her own?

▸ **At one time or another, nearly everyone needs to ask for help.** Are there ways in which you sometimes need help? Explain.

▸ Are there ways in which you feel sorry for yourself? Describe what they are. When you think about those things, how does it make you feel? What can you think about instead?

▸ When you make a choice to care about the needs of others, how do you end up seeing yourself?

▸ **While Jesus was here on earth, He forgot about himself. He took care of His needs by going to a quiet place and being still before His Father. Jesus wanted to do the will of His Father.** In what ways did Jesus forget about himself in order to help us? What are some things you can do each day in order to keep your eyes on Jesus?

Let each of you look out not only for his own interests, but also for the interests of others. Philippians 2:4 (NKJV)

Forgive me, Lord, for thinking so much about myself that I forgot about or don't even see the needs of others. Help me to notice when other people need help. Give me a heart that's willing to reach out. I want to keep my eyes on you, Jesus, and live as you lived.

I Can't Help Wondering

Todd was upstairs and not quite ready to leave when he heard the doorbell ring. A moment later Mom answered the door. Todd heard the low rumble of his dad's voice.

Taking a final swipe at his hair, he moved quietly to the top of the stairs. Sure enough, they were arguing again. Now and then Todd heard his name. *It must be about me.*

Walking on tiptoe, he went back to his room. He'd already been in the middle of too many fights. He didn't want to hear what they said.

His back against the door, Todd stood there clenching and unclenching his fists. He dreaded going downstairs. He wished it could be like the old days, when Dad lived here and all of them did things together.

Then the same old question popped into Todd's mind. He tried to push it aside, but it didn't leave. Instead, he felt tears in his eyes. He blinked, wishing the tears away, but they stayed.

Just then he heard a knock on his door. "Todd!" called his mom.

Todd brushed his arm across his eyes, grabbed his jacket, and opened the door. Mom stood in the hall with a bright smile on her face. As usual, she acted as though nothing had happened, but Todd knew better. He wished he could make everything all right for her.

"Your dad's here," she said. "Have a good time."

After a quick good-bye hug, Todd hurried down the stairs and out the door. As he climbed into the Jeep, he wished he could know Dad the way he used to, instead of just across a table in a restaurant.

Then the question returned. Todd pushed it to the back of his mind and pretended the answer didn't matter.

But it did. Somehow Todd felt lonely for his dad, even when they sat at the same table.

In the restaurant Dad started out the usual way. "Order whatever you want, okay?"

Todd asked for his usual hamburger, and Dad got his usual steak. Yet nothing seemed usual between them.

Todd wanted to blurt out everything that had happened that week, but he didn't know where to start. When Dad asked, "What have you been doing?" Todd answered, "Oh, nothing."

When Dad told about his business trip to New York, Todd wanted to hear about the Statue of Liberty and the Empire State Building. The questions stuck in his throat and he gave up.

Then Dad asked, "How's your chess club?" and Todd forgot to tell him about the good move he'd discovered. All he wanted to know was why Dad and Mom argued about him again.

As Todd finished his hamburger, Dad brought up his news. "I talked with your mom about taking you camping for a week. I want to go up in the mountains. I'll teach you to backpack and fish."

"Wow! Really?" asked Todd, hardly able to believe his ears.

"Really! Want to go?"

For Todd it was a dream come true. Camping. Fishing the trout streams. Being with Dad for a whole week.

Then the question came back again, and Todd felt shaky inside. Suddenly he couldn't stand it any longer. "Dad . . ."

Todd's tongue felt as if it were clumsy with peanut butter, but the question didn't go away. It must have stayed on his face.

"What's the matter, Todd?" Dad asked.

As the feeling of peanut butter disappeared, Todd's words tumbled out. "Do you *really* want to take me with you?"

"Of course I want to take you with me," Dad said. "Why do you ask?"

Again Todd struggled to speak. But it was something he had to know.

"Do you *really* want me along? Or are you just trying to get me away from Mom?"

Dad looked startled. "Todd, what a strange question."

Todd looked down and began kicking his foot against the table leg.

For a moment Dad was silent. When he spoke, his words came out slowly. "Don't you know how much I love you?"

Todd shook his head, blinking at the same time. He was afraid his tears would return.

"Why do you wonder about it?" asked Dad, his voice quiet.

Staring at his water glass, Todd twisted it around in circles. At last he got the words out. "Because you and Mom fight about me all the time."

"Ohhh." Dad's voice sounded so strange that Todd looked up. Dad's face looked even stranger.

Finally he drew a long breath. "Todd, I'm sorry to say it, but your mother and I seem to disagree about everything. Whether you're around or not wouldn't make any difference. We'd probably argue anyway."

Dad cleared his throat. "I'm not proud of it. I'm sorry we act that way. But that's our problem, not yours."

As Dad grew silent, Todd's gaze fell. Once again he began twisting his glass. *Dad didn't answer my question,* he thought. *Does he really want me? Does he like me the way I am? I can't help wondering.* Todd had to know, but he couldn't ask the question again.

After a few minutes, Dad spoke. "Want to see something?"

Dad opened his wallet to pictures of Todd from the time he was a little kid. "I carry these around all the time. That way I can look at you wherever I am."

Inside, Todd felt a glimmer of hope.

"Today your mom and I had a discussion because I want to take you camping," Dad said. "I'm not just trying to get you away from your mom. You mean so much to me that I want you with me."

Todd looked up and searched Dad's face. What he found there made him feel good all over.

Todd knew that Dad meant what he said.

TO **TALK** ABOUT

▸ What was the question Todd wanted to ask?

▸ Todd made a choice, whether to ask the question or keep wondering. Why was it important to his self-esteem to learn the truth?

▸ How do you know that Todd's mom and dad wanted to do the best they could for him?

▸ Todd had been hiding his feelings instead of telling his mom and dad what bothered him. Why is it important to talk about your feelings to someone who will listen and help?

▸ **When you need to talk about things that hurt you, it helps to start by saying, "I feel . . . (bad, sorry, hurt, etc.)" and finish the sentence.** Todd could have told his dad, "I feel bad because you and Mom argue about me." Is there something bothering you that you'd like to talk about? Try starting with "I feel" and finish the sentence.

▸ How do you know that Jesus feels bad when you hurt? For clues check the shortest verse in the Bible, John 11:35.

Thoughtless words can wound as deeply as any sword, but wisely spoken words can heal. Proverbs 12:18 (TEV)

Help me, Jesus, when I need to talk and ask questions about what's happening to me. When I feel bad about something, give me people who will really help me. Give me your healing. And help me remember that you're always with me to listen and understand.

Grandma's Story

Kelly was staying with her grandparents for the weekend. She liked being with them. Grandma seemed to know how she felt about things, even when Kelly didn't tell her. Though Grandma was seventy-six, she still stood tall and straight and slender.

Grandpa was shorter than Grandma, and his square hands were rough from working as a carpenter. His eyes crinkled at the corners, and he always looked ready to laugh. He liked to tease Kelly.

"Come on, we're going out for a fish dinner," he said.

Kelly grinned. Grandpa knew she didn't like fish, and she knew Grandpa and Grandma didn't care much for pizza. But they knew that Kelly liked it. She felt like laughing as she guessed they had planned a special time for her.

Sure enough, Grandpa pulled up in front of a pizza place and let Kelly and Grandma out. As they waited on the sidewalk, some of Grandma's friends came by. Grandma introduced them, leaving a boy about Kelly's age until last. "This is their son Stephen," she said.

Kelly smiled her hello to everyone, and especially to Stephen. *He looks nice,* she thought.

But then Kelly knew her smile had frozen on her lips. She felt tall and awkward, as though she were bending over to talk with him. *I must be a whole head taller than he is,* she told herself.

Suddenly every thought vanished from Kelly's mind. She couldn't come up with one thing to say. When Stephen asked how long she'd be visiting her grandparents, Kelly could hardly answer. Letting her shoulders slump, she tried to look smaller.

Kelly was relieved when Grandpa came, and the three of them went into the restaurant. While Grandpa ordered pizza, Kelly and Grandma waited in a booth.

For Kelly the fun had gone out of the day. All she could think about was the feeling of looking down on Stephen. *I'm bigger than any kid my age,* she thought with embarrassment. *I'd like to crawl in a hole and disappear forever.*

Instead of sitting straight, she slid down on the bench. She hoped no one would notice how tall she was, even when sitting.

Grandma broke into her thoughts. "Kelly, did I ever tell you how your grandfather and I met?"

Kelly shook her head. She was still thinking about Stephen and how short he was.

"When I was about twenty years old, I went to visit one of my cousins for the weekend. For Saturday night she invited a bunch of friends for a big treasure hunt."

"Where you have clues and go from place to place until you find the treasure?"

Grandma nodded. "My cousin divided us up as couples. She matched me with Andy, your grandfather. I was upset. There were two tall, good-looking boys in the group. I wanted to be with one of them."

Grandma laughed, remembering that long-ago time. Kelly knew the feeling, but she sure didn't feel like laughing about it.

"I thought I was big and awkward and at least a foot taller than Andy. I slumped my shoulders and hoped I could somehow look shorter."

Now Kelly felt uncomfortable. Once again Grandma had guessed her thoughts. Kelly straightened, sitting tall, and took a deep breath.

"But Andy teased me," Grandma went on. "He called me Skyscraper! I was hopping mad. I didn't want to go around the block with him, let alone on a treasure hunt."

Grandma smiled. "But the teams were all set. Your grandfather and I went from clue to clue. We were always just a minute or two ahead of everyone. When we came to the last clue, we were in the lead."

Kelly leaned forward, listening.

"The clue was tucked in a tin can in the hollow of a tree. When I shone the flashlight, I was tall enough to see the glint of the tin. Andy couldn't see it at all." Grandma paused.

"Go on," Kelly said.

"I thought, 'If I tell him I see it, he'll know it's because I'm taller. He'll tease me again.' "

"What happened?" asked Kelly.

"Just then I heard a noise. Another couple was close on our trail. I reached up, grabbed the can, took out one clue, and stuffed the can back in its place. We won the treasure!"

"What was it?" asked Kelly.

Grandma laughed. "A fake diamond ring and two tickets to a play. Andy had to take me out. He groaned and pretended that was no treasure. He got me to laugh about being taller than he was. It was the first time I'd ever laughed about being tall."

Kelly couldn't imagine laughing at something like that. "And you kept going together?"

A slow smile curved Grandma's lips. "I started to realize it was probably even harder for him to be short than for me to be tall—especially if he liked me. Eventually we got married. I've never been sorry. I've always known how much I mean to Andy."

"It really didn't matter? That you're taller, I mean?"

Grandma shook her head. "You come from a long line of tall people, Kelly. It's hard now, but many of the boys will catch up. A few will even pass you. If you slump your shoulders, you'll look tired or discouraged or ashamed of how you look."

Just then Grandpa set the pizza on the table. But Grandma kept talking. "If you stand up straight, you'll let people see how nice you are on the inside."

"And you'll get a good-looking husband like me." Grandpa winked.

Kelly grinned. "I'll have to think about it," she said, reaching for the pizza. But to herself she added, *Maybe that wouldn't be so bad after all.*

TO **TALK** ABOUT

▸ **Most of us have something we don't like about the way we're made.** We think we're too tall, too short, too fat, or too thin. Our nose is too long or our ears too big. Or perhaps we have a physical, emotional, or mental disability. Sometimes, as with Paula's weight (see "How Can I Like *Me*?" p. 67), there are things we can change. Other times we need to accept the way we are. Is Kelly's height something she can change or something she needs to accept?

▸ What are some things about yourself that you need to accept? Explain.

▸ What happens to your self-esteem if you keep thinking about what you don't like about yourself? Why are girls often taller than boys during their middle-school years?

▸ If tall people stand tall, what happens to their appearance? Does that give a clue about how to handle anything else you don't like about yourself? Give an example.

▸ **The Bible says that God saw you before you were born, even while you were being made.** If you don't like the way you are, what are you telling God about how He made you?

▸ What is something you *do* like about the way you're made? How does it help your self-esteem to know the strengths God has given you?

▸ Someone has said, "It's not how you look, but who you are that's important." Is that an excuse for looking sloppy or not being clean? What do you think these words really say? How can you put that idea into practice? Give your ideas.

I praise you because I am fearfully and wonderfully made; your works are wonderful, I know that full well. Psalm 139:14

Father, you know that often I don't like the way I'm made. Yet because you created me this way, I choose to accept the way I am. I choose to develop the strengths you have given me. Thank you!

How's My Mom?

They stood at the church door, ready to leave. Cheri looked at her mom, as if for the first time.

She's really pretty! Cheri thought. Mom's dark brown eyes sparkled, and her lips curved in a smile.

As Mom shook hands with Pastor Evenson, he asked, "How are you doing?"

Mom smiled again. "Fine, just fine," she said.

Yet as Mom and Cheri and two-year-old Rachel walked the short distance home, Cheri noticed the shadow in Mom's eyes. Since Dad stopped living with them, Cheri had seen that shadow of unhappiness often. She dreaded what it meant and hoped she was wrong.

As they ate lunch, Mom said, "Let's go for a bike ride." Soon they were off, Cheri on her own bike and little Rachel in the bike seat behind Mom. The September day was perfect, and Mom seemed okay.

Once, she stopped to point out the ducks on a pond. Another time she pulled up the hood on Rachel's sweat shirt to protect her from the wind. Mom had even brought treats along. After a while they sat down by a lake to eat them.

But when they got home that evening, Mom started drinking again.

Did I say something that upset her? Cheri wondered. As her mom downed one glass after another, Cheri blamed herself. *I thought I poured it all out.*

Cheri pretended that she didn't see what was happening. Yet as she watched TV, she kept count of the glasses, and her uneasiness grew. Sometimes when Mom drank, she just got sad and talked strange. Other times she acted mean.

Which way is Mom going to act this time? Cheri wondered, feeling scared.

Soon she found out. In her funny toddler way, Rachel went over to Mom and held up her bottle. Mom pushed the bottle aside.

Rachel tried again.

"Don't bother me!" snapped Mom, shoving the little girl away.

Rachel yowled. Cheri jumped up and pulled her into the kitchen. After filling her bottle, she took Rachel to the bedroom, changed her clothes, and put her to bed.

Feeling as though a giant hand twisted her insides, Cheri crept into her own bed. For a long time, she lay there, afraid to fall asleep. She thought about the last time Mom got like this.

Though the night wasn't cold, Cheri started to shiver, remembering. *Mom is so nice when she's sober—so unhappy when she's drinking.*

Now Cheri wondered as she had a hundred times, *What did I do wrong? Where are you, God? I'm so scared.*

Cheri thought about Sunday school that morning and the Bible verse her class had learned. "Let not your heart be troubled," Jesus had said. "You believe in God, believe also in Me" (NKJV).

Just thinking about the words, Cheri started to cry. Soon she pulled her blankets over her head. Afraid Mom would hear her sobs, Cheri buried her face in the pillow. " 'Let not your heart be troubled,' " she kept repeating to herself. "I believe in you, God. I believe in you, Jesus."

After a long time, Cheri stopped sobbing, but her heart still cried out, *What should I do, Jesus? What should I do?*

As she finally drifted off to sleep, Cheri wondered if she should tell someone. Just as quickly as the thought came to her mind, she tossed it out. *I don't want anyone to know how Mom acts,* she thought, filled with shame. *I'd be embarrassed to tell them.*

The next morning Mom seemed better. She had the day off, but Cheri had school. *What about Rachel?* Cheri wondered. *If I go to school, will she be okay? If I ask about it, Mom might get mad.*

When she could wait no longer, Cheri finally left for school. Off and on through the day, she thought about Rachel. The minute school was out, Cheri hurried home.

As she walked up the front sidewalk, she heard Rachel crying and broke into a run. The little girl sounded as if she'd been crying for a long time.

Bounding up the porch steps, Cheri tried to open the front door. It was locked. From somewhere Rachel still cried. Cheri's heart tugged at the sound.

Her panic growing, Cheri rattled the door. Then she ran along the porch to the front window. Peering in, Cheri saw Mom sprawled on the sofa, sound asleep. A bottle lay on the floor beside her.

Cheri felt sick. With another bound she was down the

steps, heading around the side of the house. Once again she heard Rachel. Her crying seemed closer.

Following the sound, Cheri came to the backyard. There in full sunlight was Rachel's playpen.

As Rachel saw Cheri, the little girl held up her arms and whimpered. Cheri picked her up and hugged her. When she saw Rachel's sunburned arms and face, Cheri broke into sobs.

It's all my fault! If I hadn't gone to school . . .

Still holding Rachel, Cheri sat down in the shade. Clutching the child in her arms, Cheri cried as she had never cried before.

Rachel nestled close, her arms circling Cheri's neck. Through her tears Cheri looked down at her. *Oh, God, what should I do?* This time her cry for help was a prayer.

Two words dropped into her mind: *Tell someone.* But Cheri still pushed the idea aside.

Then Rachel stirred in her arms. Gently Cheri touched the little girl's skin. It felt hot and dry with sunburn. Her eyelids and cheeks were puffy from crying. Once again Cheri's heart tugged with the pain of it.

In that moment she remembered Pastor Evenson looking at Mom and asking, "How are you doing?"

Could I talk to him? Cheri wondered.

Staggering under Rachel's weight, Cheri stood up and started walking to church.

TO **TALK** ABOUT

▸ What does it mean to say that someone has a drinking problem?

▸ What was Cheri's mom like when she wasn't drinking? How

did she change when she started to drink? Why was Cheri afraid of what her mom would do?

▶ Her mother's drinking had affected Cheri's self-esteem. What are some clues that tell you how Cheri felt about herself? Why did Cheri wonder, *What did I do wrong?*

▶ When Cheri found Rachel sunburned and crying, she said to herself, *It's all my fault.* Was what happened to Rachel really Cheri's fault? Why or why not?

▶ Cheri became an in-spite-of-it kid. She made a good choice in going to talk with Pastor Evenson. What do you think he'll do to help Cheri's mom?

▶ **If you or one of your friends needs help because of a problem like Cheri's, there are people you can talk to.** Who are they? Think of a school or Sunday school teacher, a pastor, neighbor, relative, or friend you trust. There are also groups called Alcoholics Anonymous that help people who have a problem because of drinking.

▶ **If you have hard things in your life, Jesus understands when you hurt. He wants you to ask Him for help. He wants to heal you. But you also need to talk with people you trust.**

▶ Let's fast-forward the ending of this story to a time after Cheri's mom receives help and makes changes in her life. Imagine another Sunday afternoon when she and Cheri and Rachel take their bikes and have fun. What are some things that the three of them can enjoy doing together?

He who dwells in the secret place of the Most High shall abide under the shadow of the Almighty. I will say of the Lord, "He is my refuge and my fortress; my God, in Him I will trust." Psalm 91:1–2 (NKJV)

Thank you, God, for caring about what happens to me. If I'm ever in trouble, remind me that I can always ask you for help. Help me to also talk to the right grown-up. Protect me. Take away my scared feelings and heal me. In the strong name of Jesus I pray! Thank you!

Better Than an *A*

The bus had nearly reached Adam's farm when Marty asked him, "Want to go to the game tonight? My brother said he'd give us a ride."

Adam couldn't think of anything he'd like better. The small town where he went to school had a good team this year. One more win and they'd go to sectionals.

"Sure," Adam said. "What time?"

But half an hour later he had a problem. "Sorry, but you can't go," Mom said. "You need to study."

"Aw, Mom!"

"Remember that letter about your grades? You have to do better in social studies. Last night you said you have a test tomorrow."

"I'll study right now. If I miss the game, I'll just sit and think about it. It won't do me any good to stay home."

Mom shook her head. "You've got chores first. Go call Marty and tell him you can't go."

Marty wasn't any help. "Aw, you don't need to study. I'm not going to. The test will just cover all the stuff we've been quizzed on."

Adam got off the phone feeling angry. *Stupid social stud-*

ies class! Just the same, he knew he hadn't read even half the pages.

Later, as he opened his social studies book, Adam thought about all the kids pouring into the school gym. Everyone from the whole area would be there. His friends would meet on the top bleacher.

As Adam stared out the window, the yard light glowed in the darkness. Yet in his mind Adam saw only the gym and Patrick O'Leary dribbling the ball across the court. Patrick was their team's top scorer.

Maybe I'll be just as good a player someday, Adam thought. *I'm good now. In a few more years . . .*

But if he didn't get his grades up, Mom and Dad wouldn't let him go out for basketball. Adam sighed.

When he looked down at his book, he realized he had turned pages without remembering one thing he read. Starting over, Adam did his best to concentrate. This time it began to make sense. Taking out his notebook, he outlined the material the way his teacher had shown him.

Next he made a list of things he needed to memorize. On one side of the paper he wrote the states. Opposite them, he listed their capital cities. Then he folded the paper in half and tested himself.

By the time he went to bed, Adam felt good about what he'd learned. *Bet I'll hit a winning score on that test.* He couldn't remember ever studying so hard.

The following morning Adam didn't like hearing about the terrific game he'd missed. But his good feelings returned when he took the test. Never before had he been able to finish a test so quickly, feeling sure of the answers. Only in a few places did he have trouble. With those he guessed and hoped for the best.

The next day the test came back with a large B at the top. *GREAT!* the teacher had written in bold letters. *BIG IM-PROVEMENT!*

For the first time all year, Adam could be proud of his grade. *Wait till Mom and Dad see this,* he thought.

"How did you do?" asked Marty from across the aisle.

"Got a B," Adam said, feeling good all over. "I really studied. How about you?"

"Oh, what I usually get." Marty quietly slid his test paper under a book. Before it disappeared, Adam saw his grade.

A! he thought. *Another A! I don't understand. How does Marty always do it?*

Adam liked Marty. He liked the way he never made a big thing about getting better grades. Yet just then all Adam could think about was the game he hadn't seen.

Marty went and didn't study. I missed the game and didn't get as good a grade! It's not fair!

Somehow the B didn't seem important anymore. In comparison with Marty's A, it didn't count.

What's the use? Adam asked himself. *My grades will never be as good as his. I could just as well have gone to the game.*

Adam knew that wasn't really true, but the rest of the day it was all he thought about. *I don't want to study that hard again.* Adam didn't know what he'd do the next time a test rolled around.

TO **TALK** ABOUT

▸ Give some possible reasons why Marty didn't need to study.

▸ What's more important for Adam—to compare his B with

what he's done before, or to compare his grade with Marty's A? Why do you think this story is called "Better Than an *A*"?

▸ What is Adam's long-term goal? How would it help him to think about that goal?

▸ **Most of us compare our weaknesses with someone else's strengths.** In what way do you compare the things that are hard for you with the things someone else does well? Why does that hurt your self-esteem?

▸ What are some things *you* do well? How can those things help you become an in-spite-of-it kid because you know that God has gifted you?

▸ What do you think Jesus wants Adam to be—his best or his worst? Why do you feel that way? How did Jesus give His best for us?

▸ What do you think Marty will do the next time a test comes around? Think of a new ending to this story. In the final paragraph, what words would you change?

Do your best to present yourself to God as one approved, a workman who does not need to be ashamed and who correctly handles the word of truth. 2 Timothy 2:15

Thank you, Lord, that you can help me do my best, even when things are hard for me. Help me to not compare my weaknesses with someone else's strengths. Remind me of the things I do well.

Cathy's Song

Minutes before the spring concert started, Cathy stood on the stage of the school auditorium. Behind her, the band was warming up. Scales and tuning notes blended in a swirl of sound.

As choir members started falling into line, Cathy hurried over to the side of the closed curtain. Through the narrow space between the cloth and the wall, she could see half of the audience. By now most of the seats were filled.

Starting at the front, Cathy checked each seat. As she reached the last row, she sighed. *They're not here,* she thought. *Neither Mom nor Dad came.*

With a sinking heart, Cathy crossed the stage to peer out from the other side of the curtain. Her friend Karin joined her there.

"Just a minute. Let me look," Karin said as she peered over Cathy's shoulder. "Yup! There they are! Right in the front row."

Cathy looked, too. Sure enough, there was Karin's family—her mom, dad, sister, and brother, as well as a grandpa and grandma. *And Karin isn't even singing a solo!* Cathy felt even more alone.

"Did you find your parents?" Karin asked.

Cathy shook her head and tried to swallow around the lump in her throat. Karin's parents had given Cathy a ride to school because she needed to be here early. But Mom promised that she and Dad would come in time for the concert.

Will they really? Cathy wondered. *That's what they said last time. And the time before. And the time before that.*

Again Cathy peered through the crack between the curtain and the wall. This time she checked the audience on the right side. Again she looked across each row. The farther back she went, the more desperate she felt. She dreaded coming to that last row and knowing her parents weren't there.

"See 'em?" Karin asked.

Numbly Cathy shook her head. She wished she could tell Karin how she felt. She wished Karin would hug her and say it was okay. But during the winter concert, Dad had to be out of town. Mom was at a women's meeting. Would both of them have something else to do tonight?

Cathy sighed, the despair within her growing.

Karin tugged her arm. "Come on. We have to get in line."

As Cathy found her place in the choir, her shoulders sagged. *Do Mom and Dad really love me? Do they love me enough to be here?*

"Maybe they'll still come," Karin said softly.

"The choir's first and the band's second," Cathy whispered back. "My solo's in the fourth song. I've practiced two whole months, and no one will hear me!"

"I will," said Karin, trying to cheer her up.

But Cathy couldn't even smile. *How can I sing when I just want to cry?*

Just then the curtain opened, and Cathy followed the line of singers onto the risers. In the moment before she looked at the director, she searched the rows once more. Mom and Dad still weren't there.

During the first song, Cathy sang through stiff lips. She felt angry all the way through.

Halfway into the next number, Cathy felt sorry for herself. She wished she belonged to Karin's family. As a tear slid down her cheek, Cathy froze like a statue, trying to pretend nothing was wrong.

Just before the choir started the third number, she straightened her shoulders and cleared her throat. Singing always made her feel better. Maybe no one else would understand how music seemed to well up within her. *No matter what happens, I'm going to do the best I can.*

Her solo was next. Stepping out of the choir, Cathy moved forward to the microphone. All she could think about were the words she needed to remember. As she listened to the piano introduction, she saw the lift of Mr. Lee's baton.

Cathy began to sing, and her first notes wavered. Then her voice grew stronger. As she reached for the high notes, she knew it was the best she'd ever sung. In that moment she forgot everything else. She just felt the music.

When the applause broke around her, Cathy smiled and took her bow. But she looked in only one direction. Toward the back of the auditorium.

TO **TALK** ABOUT

▸ What do you think Cathy saw at the back of the auditorium? How do you think she felt?

▸ God loves and cares for each one of us. But why do we need to know we're loved by the people we love?

▸ Maybe Cathy's parents had a good reason why they couldn't make it to the concert in time. If that's true, what should Cathy do when she talks to her parents?

▸ What happened when Cathy decided she wasn't going to feel sorry for herself? How did she become an in-spite-of-it kid?

▸ Have you ever been disappointed by someone you love? Did you tell them how you felt? Were you able to straighten it out with them? Explain.

▸ Think about the times when people you love have given you happy surprises. What were they? How can you offer happy surprises to others?

▸ **There's one person who wants to always be with you—Jesus. There's one thing that will never change—His love for you.** What does it mean to say, "Jesus is with me"? What does it mean to truly believe He *is* with you?

▸ Sometimes it's hard to *know* that Jesus is with you because you can't *feel* that He is. But there's a big truth: You don't have to count on your feelings. If you ask Him to be with you, He will be. Jesus is the best promise keeper of all. When you need to remember that, repeat these verses, or similar ones, until they seem real to you:

"I will not leave you as orphans; I will come to you." John 14:18

"I have called you friends." John 15:15b

"And surely I am with you always, to the very end of the age." Matthew 28:20b

▸ **To keep your eyes on Jesus, remember His prom-**

ises and tell Him, "Thanks for being with me!"

When I feel alone, help me, Jesus, to know that you are with me. By faith I choose to believe that, even when I can't feel it. Help me to also know your love through my mom, dad, sister, brother, grandparents, and other people who are important to me. Thank you!

A Present for Chris

Chris was in his room when the doorbell rang. The sudden jolt to his insides warned him. All through supper he had felt terrible about what he did. Had someone found out?

Quietly he opened his door a crack and listened. It was Mr. Roberts talking to Dad. Chris's misery grew.

"Chris!" The sound of Dad's voice came up the stairway.

Maybe I can pretend I'm not here, Chris thought. *Maybe I can hide in the closet.* Yet he knew that Dad would find him later.

Again Dad called, and Chris started down the stairs. With every step his guilty feelings exploded like a firecracker. He dreaded the look he'd find in his father's eyes.

Dad had invited Mr. Roberts into the living room. *Uh-oh! Big trouble!* Chris thought.

"What were you doing this afternoon?" Dad asked him.

Chris fixed his gaze on the carpet. "Oh, I don't know. I played ball and then came home."

"Mr. Roberts tells me you broke the antenna of the car they had parked on the street. His wife saw you and told him when he got home. Is that true?" asked Dad.

With his foot Chris traced a circle on the rug. He wanted to lie but knew he couldn't get away with it. Finally he nodded.

"Why, Chris?" Dad sounded puzzled. "Why did you do it?"

"I was mad," Chris said. The words choked in his throat. "Mad at the ump. He didn't call the game fair, and we lost. He made it look like it was all my fault."

Chris stopped. He couldn't tell Dad all of it. He'd wanted to lash out at anything he could. It was such an awful day that he wondered if *anyone* cared what happened to him.

"What should you say to Mr. Roberts?" Dad asked.

Slowly Chris looked up. "I guess I should say I'm sorry." He really meant it, but he felt so ashamed that it didn't sound that way.

"I forgive you," Mr. Roberts said. "But I think you should talk to my wife. She uses that car for work."

His feet dragging the whole way, Chris followed Mr. Roberts to his house. He'd known Mrs. Roberts since he was a little kid. When he was five or six, he and the other kids often stopped there for cookies. That was a long time ago, and now Chris felt ashamed to look her in the eyes.

"I'm sorry I broke your antenna," he said, stumbling over the words. "It was a stupid thing to do."

"I know you're sorry," said Mrs. Roberts. "And I forgive you."

Chris looked up. "You forgive me? You aren't mad?"

"Yes, I forgive you. And I'm not mad. I'm disappointed about what you did, but I'm not mad."

"How come?" Chris asked, then felt surprised he'd spoken the words.

"Because I've done wrong things in my own life," answered Mrs. Roberts. "And I've learned some things the hard way. When I ask forgiveness, Jesus *does* forgive me. He not only forgives, He forgets about it."

"Forgets about it?"

"He loves me as though I've never done anything wrong."

Chris wasn't sure about this God stuff. He'd like to believe she was right, but a part of him still wondered, *How can God or anyone else forget what I did?*

In that moment Chris just wanted to get out of there, but Mrs. Roberts interrupted his thoughts. "I believe you mean it when you ask forgiveness. And I forgive you. As far as I'm concerned, everything is wiped clean between us. It's as though nothing ever happened. Okay?"

"Okay!" answered Chris, filled with relief.

"But there's one more thing," Mrs. Roberts said. "When Jesus forgives us, He wants us to turn from what we've done wrong and live a different way. How would you like to show me that you want to live a different way? Not breaking antennas, I mean?"

Chris was puzzled. It felt good to be forgiven, but he had no idea how to do what she asked. And right now, Mrs. Roberts wanted an answer.

Forced into thinking about it, Chris came up with something. "I guess I should pay for the antenna."

Mrs. Roberts agreed. "It would help you remember that you don't want to do the same thing again. What would be a fair amount of work to make up for a new antenna?"

Oh brother! thought Chris. He could sure think of things he'd rather do than work. But like it or not, he knew Mrs. Roberts was right.

Together they decided Chris would mow the Robertses' lawn until the money was paid. The next afternoon Chris was back, feeling glad that Mrs. Roberts had forgiven him. She even treated him like old times. Yet Chris wished he could go play ball with his friends.

Making quick sweeps around the yard, Chris wondered if he could finish in time to meet his friends at the park. He was halfway through mowing when Mrs. Roberts came out of the house and tapped him on the shoulder.

"That's not good enough," she said, pointing to the hunks of grass Chris had missed.

Chris felt anger well up within. The fact that she was right made things worse. But Chris didn't have any choice. Swinging the mower around, he went back over the hunks.

As he started a new section of lawn, Chris glanced back to where he'd been. To his surprise, the grass looked smooth and even. When Chris finished, he checked it again. This time he felt proud of his work. The yard looked great except for the ragged edges that needed trimming by hand.

Chris started to the door to tell Mrs. Roberts he was finished. Halfway there, he thought about the ragged places and stopped. *I don't have to do it,* he told himself. *She didn't tell me to do the trimming.*

Then came a thought he couldn't push aside. *But she didn't have to forgive me.*

Chris stood there, trying to decide. *If I don't do it, I can go play ball.*

Then he remembered last night—how ashamed he'd been, and how good it felt when Mrs. Roberts forgave him. *It was like she gave me a present.*

Chris found the clippers in the garage and trimmed around the flower beds. As he headed for the house a second time, Mrs. Roberts came out with a plate of cookies.

Wow! Chris thought. *Things really are okay again!*

TO **TALK** ABOUT

▸ **None of us feel good about ourselves if we need to be forgiven by God or someone else.** How did Chris feel after he broke the antenna? When did that feeling change?

▸ "Confessing your sins" means to say you're sorry for what you did. But it also means to be sorry—truly sorry. Not just sorry that you got caught. What's the difference between the two?

▸ What words did Chris use to ask forgiveness?

▸ What words did Mrs. Roberts use to offer Chris the gift of forgiveness? What reason did she give for forgiving him?

▸ Mrs. Roberts also told Chris that because he asked for forgiveness and she gave it, everything was okay between them. Why was it important for Chris to know that?

▸ How does God see us after we ask forgiveness and He gives it to us? What has happened to our sin? Who made that possible? How?

▸ How did Chris show that he not only was sorry for what he did, but wanted to live a different way?

Everyone has sinned and is far away from God's saving presence. But by the free gift of God's grace all are put right with him through Christ Jesus, who sets them free. Romans 3:23 (TEV)

Jesus, I'm sorry about the wrong things I've done. (Tell Jesus what they are.) I ask your forgiveness. Thank you that when I ask, you do forgive me. Thanks that in your eyes I'm a new kid! I ask for your power to live in a new way.

Tell Me More

For as long as Jason could remember, he had been good with a basketball. As he showered and dressed, he relived the game.

At the end of the first quarter, the Pirates were trailing. By the half they were still behind, with the gap narrowing. Then Jason hit a winning streak. As his teammates fed the ball to him, he dribbled in for lay-ups. One ball after another went in. Whenever he couldn't break free, he tried for long shots. Even those swished through the net.

Now, with an easy grin on his face, Jason accepted the congratulations all around him. Yet as the locker room emptied out, he stayed behind. For some reason the victory seemed empty. Jason couldn't understand it.

I've worked a long time for this day, he thought, sitting down on a bench. But a strange restlessness stirred inside him. All the ways he had succeeded didn't seem enough.

Elbows on his knees, Jason stared at the floor. *What's wrong with me? Why do I feel so empty inside?*

Just then Rusty came into the locker room. "Great game, Jason!"

Rusty was the equipment manager. While everyone else

117

wanted to be out on the court playing, Rusty made sure they had whatever equipment they needed. "Hey, what's the matter?" he asked.

With anyone else Jason would have said, "Nothing! Nothing at all!" But he liked Rusty. The shortest boy in their grade, Rusty had gotten his nickname because of his red hair and freckles. On the outside, he seemed exactly opposite from the hero Jason thought himself to be.

Then a couple of months ago, Jason started noticing Rusty. *No one pays any attention to him,* Jason thought. *No one even thanks him. How come he seems to like what he's doing?*

Rusty always seemed to be carrying something—the basketballs or whatever someone else forgot. Rusty did his job without saying much. Yet when the team needed help, he was always there.

Now, as Jason faced him, he wondered about it again. "How come you're equipment manager?"

" 'Cause I like basketball," Rusty said.

"Then why don't you play?"

"Well, I tried." Rusty dropped onto the bench next to Jason. "I used to dream about playing like you. But I didn't make the team."

"That's a tough break."

"Yeah." Rusty's voice was matter-of-fact. "I used to feel that way. But I sure wouldn't say it to someone like you."

"You don't feel bad anymore?"

Rusty shook his head. "Not anymore."

Jason was curious. "How come? I'd hate it if I couldn't play."

"Well, I'm not sure you'd understand." Rusty sounded as if he was feeling his way.

"Sure I would."

"Well . . ." Rusty said again. "It has to do with how God made me."

God talk! thought Jason, ready to shut out any words he didn't want to hear, the way he always did. Restless now, he stuffed clothes in his gym bag.

But Rusty kept talking. "God could have made me just like you. It would have been great if He had. But He didn't. This is the way God made me."

Standing up, Rusty spread his arms wide. Like a clown, he made a joke of it. "This is me—all there is!"

Jason laughed with him. "I've never met anyone else like you!"

At the same time Jason was curious. He knew all the good things about being what he was. The tallest boy in their grade. The best basketball player. The guy all the other kids wanted to be.

Jason wondered about it. *How can Rusty make a joke of what he* isn't? Yet Jason felt afraid to ask.

Rusty looked at Jason's face and guessed. "Sounds stupid, huh? You think I'm just pretending to like the way I am?"

Jason was smart enough to be embarrassed. "Well, now that you mention it."

But Rusty spoke with a sureness in his voice that startled Jason. "I feel good about who I am because I know how much God loves me."

Jason swore. "You're crazy!"

"No, I'm not." Rusty was unshaken.

Grabbing his gym bag, Jason stood up and started for the door. Halfway there, he stopped and turned around. In spite of the biggest win of his life, he still felt empty inside. He couldn't push that emptiness away.

"How do you know God loves you?" Jason asked. "What gives you that big idea?"

Rusty spoke quickly, as though knowing he wouldn't have another chance. "Because Jesus died for me. He loves me so much that He died on a cross. He loves you, too, Jason, the same way."

For a long moment Jason stood there, feeling embarrassed again. He couldn't decide whether to keep on going or turn around. Finally he set down his gym bag and came back.

"Tell me more, Rusty," he said. "Tell me more."

TO **TALK** ABOUT

▸ If Rusty *didn't* like the way God created him, why would he find it hard to reach out to Jason?

▸ Who gave Rusty the power to talk with Jason, even though Jason laughed at what he said?

▸ **God uses other people to help us feel loved and good about ourselves. God also gives us the best reason of all for self-esteem.** Why did Rusty feel good about who he is?

▸ What's the difference between feeling strong and good about yourself and being conceited? How can you keep from getting conceited?

▸ You may be the only person who's able to talk with the kids around you each day. Do some of them need to know Jesus? How can you pray for them? Who will give you the words to say? How do you know?

▸ Or maybe you're like Jason and feel an empty space inside. If you're wondering what it means to know Jesus as your

Savior and Lord, think about this:

1) **Jesus loves you.** "For God loved the world so much that he gave his only Son, so that everyone who believes in him may not die but have eternal life." (John 3:16, TEV)

2) **Jesus died for your sin.** "God has shown us how much he loves us—it was while we were still sinners that Christ died for us!" (Romans 5:8, TEV)

3) **Tell Jesus you're sorry for your sin.** Ask forgiveness. "If we say we have no sin, we deceive ourselves, and there is no truth in us. But if we confess our sins to God, he will keep his promise and do what is right: he will forgive us our sins and purify us from all our wrongdoing." (1 John 1:8–9, TEV)

4) **Ask Jesus to be your Savior and Lord.** " 'Everyone who calls upon the name of the Lord will be saved.' " (Romans 10:13) When you ask Jesus for salvation, you receive it.

If you would like to invite Jesus to come into your life, pray these words:

Thank you, Jesus, that you love me. Thank you for dying for me. I'm sorry for my sin and ask you to forgive me. I ask you to be my Savior and Lord. Thank you for my salvation, and that it begins right now!

If you have prayed this prayer, it's important that you tell other Christians what you believe. It will make your choice for Jesus seem more real to you.

From the Pitcher's Mound

Jennifer plopped down on the bench, rested her chin on her hands, and stared at the ground. *What's happening to me, anyway?* she asked herself.

Only last week she had pitched a no-hit game for her team, the Cardinals. Each time she threw the ball, it went exactly where she wanted. When they won, the coach and team hugged her, saying over and over, "Great game, Jenny!"

But today—wow! What a difference! First she'd let a player walk. Next she fumbled a fly. Finally the other team batted a home run, bringing in three players and ending the game.

Now Jennifer felt dusty and tired. A shower would help, but it wouldn't wash off the feeling that she had let down her team. That would probably never leave.

Taking a deep breath, Jennifer started toward the parking lot. *Days like this I hate myself. What's wrong with me?*

Partway to the car, Jennifer stopped and waited for her family to catch up. Just then she heard someone talking on the other side of a van.

"She's too sure of herself," the voice said. "She's letting her game slide."

A low mumble answered, and Jennifer couldn't pick out the words. Then the first voice spoke again. "If Coach had let me in, I would have turned it around. I'm a better pitcher any day."

Tara! thought Jennifer. *My old friend Tara! Or my used-to-be friend. Used-to-be before she wanted to be a pitcher!*

Jennifer's anger churned. *If that's my friend, I don't need an enemy!*

She felt like stomping around to the other side of the van. *I'd like to walk right up to Tara and tell her what I think. I'd make her take back every word!*

Losing the game was bad enough. Now this! Jennifer felt completely wiped out.

A moment later Jennifer's parents caught up with her. "You tried your hardest," said Mom, giving her a hug. Usually she and Dad could cheer Jennifer up, but they didn't seem to help today. Jennifer felt like a softball splitting apart at the seams.

The next time her team played, Jennifer discovered the last game wasn't over. She saw kids look at her, then glance away without meeting her eyes. Once she heard a whisper, "Taking her game for granted."

Suddenly Jennifer knew. Tara had started a whispering campaign.

An anger unlike any Jennifer had ever known shot through her. Whenever she thought of Tara, the sparks fanned into flames. Her feelings added fuel to the fire.

That anger still blazed when Jennifer took the pitcher's mound. As she faced the first batter, Jennifer bit her lip and tried to stay calm. Yet it wasn't long until the ump shouted, "Ball four!"

The second batter got off a long hit between second and

third. The crowd groaned. Jennifer knew she was losing her grip.

Taking a deep breath, she tried again. The windup. The pitch. Oh no! The batter hit a home run! The roar from the crowd sounded deafening.

"See? You're no good!" it seemed to say.

Jennifer wasn't surprised when the coach called her out. Nor was she surprised to see Tara take her place. Jennifer's anger flared up, this time like a forest fire.

Sitting on the bench, elbows on her knees, Jennifer stared straight ahead. As the Cardinals fell further behind the Blue Jays, she watched every move of the game. Yet her thoughts churned round and round.

She felt desperate. Lately Jennifer hadn't prayed much, but she began now. Even so, her prayers didn't seem to get off the ground. Something seemed in the way between her and God.

The second inning passed. Then the third. Jennifer still sat on the bench. By the beginning of the fourth, she started sorting out her choices. One word dropped into her mind.

Forgive? You gotta be kidding, God. Tara was the one who started it.

Through the first half of that inning, Jennifer argued with herself and with God. *See? I am a better pitcher. Tara's losing the game. They're three runs ahead of us. We might never catch up!*

But the word stayed in her mind. *Forgive? You want* me *to forgive Tara? I don't* want *to forgive her!*

One minute Jennifer felt ashamed of herself. The next minute she decided she didn't want to change the way she felt. *If I stop being mad, it will seem like Tara was right.*

Out on the field the game wasn't going well. By now the

Blue Jays were four runs ahead with bases loaded. Until the last game, the Cardinals hadn't lost all season.

Then a thought struck Jennifer. *Here I sit, wanting Tara to lose so I look better. I'm almost rooting for the other team!*

Forgive? Suddenly Jennifer knew what choice to make. Eyes wide open, she stared ahead, praying silently. She used only seven words. "Jesus, in your name I forgive her."

In the next moment, Jennifer felt the weight she'd carried all week drop off her back. "Yaaaay!" she called out the next time something went right. But it was more than a cheer for the Cardinals. She was cheering herself on.

At the top of the fifth the Blue Jays came to bat. "Jenny!" called the coach. "Go on in."

This time the ball felt sweet in Jennifer's hands. Thoughts of Tara were gone. Thoughts of how good she herself might look fell away. Even the crowd didn't seem important.

Glove high above her head, Jennifer snagged the ball, then caught the catcher's signal. *I'll do my best,* she thought. *But I just want to play ball.*

Facing the batter, Jennifer wound up. *It's just a game,* she told herself. *Just a game.*

The ball looked great going across the plate.

TO **TALK** ABOUT

▸ What did Jennifer mean when she decided, "I just want to play ball"? What had changed in her thinking?

▸ **In-spite-of-it kids are not stopped by the hard things they face. Instead, they look to Jesus and follow His example.** What example did He give us about forgiving others?

‣ If you forgive someone who hurt you, does that mean the person was right in what he or she did?

‣ Forgiveness gives you a way to stop hurting and go on with your life. If you want to feel good about yourself, you have no choice but to forgive those who hurt you. When she chose to forgive Tara, Jennifer prayed in the strong name of Jesus. Why do those words have special power?

‣ When Jennifer forgave Tara, she felt she no longer carried a heavy weight. **You may forgive someone and not "feel" any different. Yet your prayer of forgiveness still counts.** How do you know?

‣ Name some of the people that Jesus forgave. Why do you suppose He forgave them?

‣ Sometimes when a person hurts you, it's important to talk with that person about it. Other times it makes matters worse to say something. Do you think Jennifer should talk with Tara about the things she said? Why or why not?

‣ Whether Jennifer's team won or lost, Jennifer won something. What was it?

[Jesus said,] "If you forgive anyone his sins, they are forgiven; if you do not forgive them, they are not forgiven." John 20:23

Jesus, when someone hurts me, I want to hate that person. Yet even on the cross you prayed, "Father, forgive them." Because of what you did, I forgive the person who hurt me. Take away my bitter and angry feelings. Thank you!

Anya's Dream

Anya's workout time that morning had been shot through with glory. Though there were no windows, it seemed that sunlight washed the gym. When she came down off the uneven parallel bars, her gymnastics coach cheered her on. "You've got it, Anya!"

Now she was back after school, making sure of every part of her routine. She wanted nothing to distract her from the perfection she'd like to achieve.

With a flying run Anya grabbed hold of the lower bar. Up, over, beat, twist. As she worked out, she sensed rather than saw that people had stopped and turned to watch. Yet she kept on, sure in her timing, holding her concentration. If she won at the meet tomorrow, who knows how far she could go?

With a final twist, Anya was on the mat, arms stretched high above her head, her spirit soaring.

The applause came. "Perfect, Anya! Absolutely perfect!" called her coach. "Now take a break. Go home and get a good night's sleep. You're ready for the meet."

She knew he was right. She was tired, yet . . .

"Just one more time," she answered.

Taking her first position, Anya poised her body, letting the routine go through her mind. Then she took a deep breath.

The run came easy. She reached out, grabbed the bar, swung up into a handstand. Down, under, swing, reach.

Not quite right, Anya told herself. Somehow her timing was off, and she fought to recover. Up, over, beat, reach . . .

The next moment Anya felt the floor coming up. Instinctively she reached out, and her left hand took the fall. Pain shot through her arm, sucked down like a giant wave, and washed over her body. Then her world went black.

Several hours later, Anya looked up from a hospital bed. She seemed surrounded by bright light. Her mom stood at the side of the bed, her coach nearby.

Have they been crying? wondered Anya. *Coach Sanders wouldn't. He'd never cry.* She drifted off again, then came back.

I don't like the look on their faces, she thought. But her eyes felt weighted. She couldn't seem to keep a thought in her mind. Again she drifted off, then opened her eyes.

Have I been crying? she wondered this time. *What's wrong?*

Then Anya felt the cast on her hand and arm, and the shock went through her. *I don't want to ask,* she thought. *If I don't ask, maybe it won't be true.* She pushed the question to the back of her mind, trying to avoid it.

But she couldn't avoid her mother's eyes. Mom reached out and pushed the hair back from Anya's forehead. "Take it easy, Annie. I love you," she said.

Annie! Anya felt sick all through. *Mom hasn't called me Annie since I was a little kid. That's what she called me when she put me on her lap, washed my scraped knees, and kissed the bandages. . . .*

No longer could Anya escape the question. "What happened?" she asked aloud.

Coach Sanders took her good hand. "Sorry, Anya. I saw you going, and I couldn't reach you in time—"

It's bad, Anya thought. *Really bad.* But she couldn't quite take it in yet. Her eyes felt too heavy.

Anya drifted off to sleep, but a few hours later, she came wide awake. This time she had no choice but to face what had happened. A broken wrist. Not just one bone, but two had been shattered and crushed. Yes, a specialist had operated on it. Yes, he had done all he could. But . . .

Like a little child she whimpered. Tears streamed down her cheeks. With every waking moment, Anya felt questions gnaw inside her. *Will I ever be able to work on the uneven parallel bars again? Will my wrist be strong enough for handstands? Will I ever compete again?*

At night the questions haunted her, questions she was afraid to ask, until one day she knew she must.

Her doctor shook his head. "I don't know, Anya. I wish I could tell you something different. Yet it would be worse if I said everything is going to be okay. One day you might find out I lied to you. I have to be honest in telling you it's the worst break I've seen, and I've seen a lot."

He didn't have to say more. Anya remembered her mom's expression when she first woke up. She remembered how Coach Sanders had looked. She couldn't escape what she had seen in their eyes.

It can't be true, God, can it? You wouldn't let this happen!

It had been a long time since Anya talked with God, but now she had plenty to tell Him. *You're supposed to be a God of love. How can you do this to me?* Each morning she woke up wanting to shake her fist at God.

When she left the hospital, Anya returned to the apartment where she lived with her mother. One day when her mom was gone, Anya shouted her rage. "God, I wanted to be a champion gymnast! How can you wreck my life this way?"

The sound of her words seemed to bounce back at her. The apartment walls closed in around her, but the questions would not stop. "Why, God, why? Why *me*?"

In the silence that came, there were no answers. Instead, the silence seemed to bleed with Anya's pain.

The next morning she got up early, the way she used to. Every day she went into the gym and watched the others work out. More than once her coach tried to get her off the bench.

"C'mon, Anya," he said. "Come over here and give tips to the others. Tell them how to improve."

Each time Anya shook her head, telling herself, *He's just trying to make me feel better. I'm not really needed.* Then a deeper thought plagued her. *If I can't be a gymnast anymore, why should I help someone else?*

As the days went on, Anya's anger and discouragement grew. Then one morning her coach found her outside the gym, trying to hide her tears. This time he made no request for help. His voice was soft, but there was steel running through it.

"Anya, I taught you to be a champion. You're not acting like one." Whirling around, he returned to the gym.

Afraid to face her own feelings, Anya fled. *I don't have to go back,* she told herself. *I'll just stay away.*

But that night she had a dream. Anya saw herself poised, standing ready for her routine. As she started to run, her feet bit into the floor. Faster, faster. Grab the bar. Up, over, under, twist. Reach out, up to a perfect handstand. Down, under, up. Another flip. Then her feet hit the mat. Standing with up-stretched arms, she waited for the applause. It thundered around her.

Anya woke up crying. She pulled the blanket over her head. Cushioning her left wrist with her pillow, she cried until her body shook. *It's in me, isn't it, God? Will I always want to be a gymnast?*

Anya didn't know the answer, but suddenly she felt a still-ness within. Something inside had changed.

Pushing back the blankets, Anya dressed, said good-bye to Mom, and started for the gym. As she opened the door, she made her decision. *Okay, God. If I can't be a champion gymnast, I'll be the best coach there ever was.*

With her head high, Anya walked over and stood near the uneven parallel bars. When she decided something, Anya meant it.

TO **TALK** ABOUT

‣ Why was Anya afraid to face the fact that her wrist was broken?

‣ After something difficult happens, people often feel angry with God. What happened when Anya went beyond being angry *at* God and started talking *with* Him about her feelings?

‣ How did Anya choose between feeling sorry for herself and going on with her life?

‣ **When it becomes impossible to reach a goal, it often helps to substitute something similar.** As

Anya works toward a new goal, what achievements might make her happy?

▸ It's good to have dreams about accomplishing something worthwhile if you keep those dreams in balance and don't let them control you. How had Anya's dream of being a gymnast started to control her?

▸ **If you are open to it, God will show you what He wants you to be.** Sometimes kids think that anything God wants would be exactly what they *don't* want. Instead, **if God calls you to do something, He will give you the desire to do it.** If you don't know what God wants you to do, why is it important to ask God to show you?

▸ Why is it important to work toward a goal, even if you don't always achieve everything you hope? What is a goal you're trying to reach?

▸ When Jesus was twelve years old, He knew what His heavenly Father wanted Him to do. What did Jesus tell His earthly parents? For a big clue see Luke 2:49.

I have learned to be content whatever the circumstances.
Philippians 4:11

It's hard to be happy, to be content, Lord, if things aren't going the way I want. Help me to turn away from feeling sorry for myself and be what you want me to be. Give me a big dream, God, about how you want to use my life. Then show me how to reach the goals you give me.

I'm Different

"I want to go," said Jamal.

"I *don't* want you to go," answered his father.

Jamal looked around the supper table, wondering if he could get help from his older brother, Nicky, or his younger sister, Elise. Right now neither of them looked ready to come to his rescue.

"Jamal, why do you want to go to this video party?" asked Mom.

"It'll be fun," he answered. "It's fun to be with the other kids."

"That's a good reason," said Dad. "But the last time you went to Ty's house, you saw a video we didn't want you to see. This one's no better."

"Aw, Dad, all my friends are gonna see it. If I don't, I won't know what to talk about at school."

"You'll feel out of it," Mom said.

Jamal turned to her, surprised that Mom seemed to be on his side. "Right! All the other parents are letting their kids go. If I don't see the video, I'll be different from everyone else."

"Hmm." Thinking about it, Dad stroked his beard. "I wonder if our family is different in other ways?"

"You bet," Nicky answered. "I'm different, too. I don't get to stay up as late as my friends."

"Maybe we should all think about this," Mom said. "Let's see what we come up with by supper tomorrow night."

When Jamal went to school the next morning, he looked for ways his family was different. *Maybe I can still talk Dad into letting me go to the party.*

Instead, he started thinking about one kid after another and how they looked. In math he saw all different shades of hair and skin. Some kids were tall and others short. Some were fat and others thin.

In gym class he noticed differences in ability. As the kids played volleyball, some of them always seemed to hit the ball into the air or smash it over the net. Other kids never did.

At the end of the day, he stood at his locker, ready to go home. Around him, kids called to each other. "See ya, J.J.!" Or "Hey, Frog, coming over to my house tonight?" Almost everyone had a different name.

But late that afternoon when Mom called him in for supper, Jamal thought of still another way his family was different. It would take him longer than other kids to get back out to play. During supper his family always talked about what had happened that day.

Jamal decided to put that time to good use. *Maybe I've got enough ammunition to change Dad's mind,* he thought as he took a big bite of his hamburger.

Partway through the meal, Dad asked, "Well, what did you come up with? What are some ways our family is different?"

Jamal started off. "When the parents of other kids drive us somewhere, they almost always play rock music. You listen to a Christian station or classical stuff. Kids think I have a nutty family."

Elise chimed in. "I'm different 'cause we go to church and some of the kids don't."

Atta girl! thought Jamal. *I'm gonna get my way yet.*

"I'm different because lots of my friends are good in sports," Nicky said. "But I'm better in music."

Mom stood up and brought more hot rolls to the table. "I'm different because I turn down promotions instead of taking a job where I'd have to travel. If I took the promotions, I couldn't work while you're in school and be home when you're home."

Uh-oh! Jamal felt uneasy now. *Maybe this isn't gonna work after all.*

Dad pushed back his chair. "I'm different because I choose to be honest in business. A lot of people don't."

Suddenly Jamal realized he wasn't going to get his way. In his disappointment he wanted to lash out and hurt Dad. "I'm different because this family wants to gab and gab and gab," he said. "Other kids get back out right after supper. They can do whatever they want."

But somehow his words didn't sound as angry as they could have. As Jamal spoke, he realized he really did like the times the family talked around the table.

"That's right. We *are* different," Dad said. "But isn't there at least one way every person on earth is different from everyone else?"

Jamal didn't want to meet Dad's eyes or answer his question. Jamal just wanted to escape outside. Another question had dropped into his mind. Maybe if he got away from the table he could push it aside. He sure didn't want to tell anyone what he was wondering. After all, what would other kids think?

But in the days that followed, Jamal's question didn't go

away. Every now and then it came back, and he started wondering again. *Is it sometimes* good *to be different?*

TO **TALK** ABOUT

▸ Some kids act different and do stupid things because they want attention and don't know how to get it in good ways. Describe some ways in which you've seen this happen.

▸ Other times kids feel different because they refuse to do something that is wrong or would hurt them. Have you needed to make that choice? What happened?

▸ Jamal felt different because his parents expected him to make good choices. How would it hurt Jamal if his mom or dad never cared about the choices he made? Why?

▸ How would you answer Jamal's question, "Is it sometimes *good* to be different?" How can feeling different from other kids sometimes protect you?

▸ If it bothers you to be different, you're probably afraid of what other kids think. If you're afraid of what other kids think, how will it affect the choices you make?

▸ **It's okay to be different when it's for a good reason.** Can you think of ways you and your family are different for good reasons?

▸ How was Jesus different from any other person who ever lived?

[The Lord says,] "I, even I, am He who comforts you. Who are you that you should be afraid of a man who will die, and of the son of a man who will be made like grass?" Isaiah 51:12 (NKJV)

Jesus, I'm afraid of being different. I'm afraid of what other kids think. Help me remember that it's your approval that counts. Thank you that it's okay to be different for a good reason. When I need to follow you, help me stand up and be counted.

What Should I Do?

For a long time Janie had wanted to be friends with Sheila. Sheila told funny stories. She seemed sure of herself. She and the girls who hung around with her always seemed to have something to do.

Janie, on the other hand, felt lonely. She didn't have any close friends. Every day felt the same.

What could I do to make Sheila like me? Janie wondered. More than once she had asked herself that question. So far she hadn't come up with any answer.

Then one July morning, as Janie was on her way to get groceries for Mom, Sheila caught up with her. "Where you going?" she asked.

Janie felt glad Sheila wanted to talk. It didn't sound very exciting to pick up a gallon of milk, but that didn't seem to bother Sheila. "If you're headed that way, let's get a sundae."

That was another thing Janie had noticed about Sheila. She always seemed to have money. Just last week Sheila had worn three new tops.

A few days later, Janie met Sheila's friend Colleen. Janie had been right—Sheila *did* think of things to do. But now and then she said things Janie didn't understand. Sheila and Colleen laughed, and Janie didn't understand why. It made her uneasy. But most of the time she liked being with them. Best of all, she started to feel she belonged.

Then one hot afternoon, Sheila gave Janie a call. "Wanna do something?"

"What's it gonna be?" Janie asked.

For the first time Sheila sounded as if she didn't have a plan. "Oh, I don't know," she said. "We'll find something. Meet you outside the ice cream store, okay?"

For some reason Janie felt uneasy, the way she had when Sheila and Colleen laughed together. But Janie pushed her uneasiness to the back of her mind and felt glad she'd been asked to go.

"Colleen needs a new swimsuit," Sheila said when they met.

There was only one place to go for that—The Fashion Rack. As they left the hot sidewalk for the cool store, Sheila moved closer to Janie. "Colleen doesn't have enough money for the swimsuit," she said in a low voice. "We're gonna help her."

"What do you mean?" Janie asked. "I don't have much money, either."

"That's not what I'm saying." Sheila sounded as though she thought Janie wasn't very smart.

Startled, Janie stared at her. "Hey, count me out!" She turned, ready to walk out the door.

"Not so fast," Sheila said. "You like being along, don't you? Stick with us, and you'll have lots of fun."

Janie knew that was true. Already she'd had good times with Sheila and her friends.

"Tell you what," Sheila said. "Instead of getting a swimsuit for Colleen, let's get something for you today. What do you want?"

Again Janie stared at Sheila, not liking what she heard. That wasn't Janie's way of thinking. She seldom got things she wanted, only what she needed. And she didn't go into a store thinking, *This is what I'm going to take.*

"What do I want?" Janie asked.

"Sure," answered Sheila, still in a low voice. "What do you want? Look around."

Well, Janie thought. *It won't hurt to look. But I won't take anything.*

The girls spread out, moving throughout the store. Janie started looking through a rack of jackets. Sure enough, there was just the jacket she'd like to have. She glanced at the price tag and knew that was out.

From there she went to the jeans. She hadn't bought a pair in what seemed forever. *Maybe I deserve them,* Janie thought.

She pushed away the idea, wishing it hadn't entered her head. But at the next rack she saw a top just like one of the new tops Sheila had worn. *I wonder. . .*

Janie didn't finish the thought, even to herself.

A moment later Sheila was at her side. "Everybody does it," she said as though there hadn't been a break in the conversation. "You wanna be like the rest of us, don't you?"

Sure, Janie thought, then hated herself.

Sheila moved closer and lowered her voice. "I'll tell you how."

As a clerk came to help them, Sheila said, "Right now we're just looking, thank you."

The clerk moved away, and Sheila began talking again. Soon Janie knew the plan. She felt scared inside, but she listened, knowing she wouldn't really do what Sheila said.

Sheila started edging away. "I'll give you the signal."

"Hey, wait!" Now Janie was more than scared. Inside her mind, a tug-of-war was going on. One part of Janie wanted the top. The other part knew it was wrong.

I'd have to save my allowance a long time to get it, she told herself.

From three racks away Sheila gave the signal. Seeing her, Janie froze. *What should I do?* she asked herself. She looked down, not wanting to meet Sheila's glance.

If I take it, will I get caught? Janie wondered. Then she came back to the same question. *What should I do?*

TO **TALK** ABOUT

▸ What do you think Janie did? Give reasons for your answer.

▸ Why did Janie want to be Sheila's friend? Why did she like being part of that group?

▸ **When someone is lonely or has poor self-esteem, it can be more tempting to do something wrong.** How did Janie's thinking change after she entered the store?

▸ When you make a good or bad choice, there are logical consequences. If Janie steals the top, what do you think will happen? What kind of consequences will there be?

▸ If Janie steals the top and gets away with it, what will God think about what she did? How will Janie feel about herself?

▸ **A friend who is really a friend won't ask you to do something that hurts you. If kids pressure you to do something wrong, what can you do about it?**

▸ Some other time Janie's problem might be different. If Sheila wants her to steal, what else might she pressure Janie to do?

▸ Deep down, there's something that Janie really needs—a place to belong. **Jesus is the only one who can truly meet her deepest needs and yours. If you don't know Him, you may have a longing and a loneliness deep inside** (See "Tell Me More," page 117).

▸ Jesus also wants to give us *human* friends with whom we belong. If you need friends, ask Jesus for kids who will help you live as He wants. Ask in the strong name of Jesus and thank Him right now, while you wait to see what He does.

Jesus, I want to be liked, and it's easy to go along with what other kids do. Show me how to say no so strongly that kids don't bother me again. Give me Christian friends who will help and support me in living as you want. Thanks, Jesus!

When sinners tempt you, don't give in. Proverbs 1:10 (TEV)

Bear Paw Clodhoppers

His brother and sisters surrounded Lars in the farmhouse kitchen. It was his older brother, Anders, who started it all. Looking at the boots Lars wore, Anders started laughing. "Remember that five-hundred-pound bear we saw? Remember the size of his paws? You're wearing bear paw clodhoppers!"

Lars swallowed hard. *Bear paw clodhoppers! What could be worse?* Lars tried to hide his feet out of sight under his chair.

But his younger sister, Tina, pointed to his long fingers. "Wow, Lars! You not only have big feet. Your hands are GIGANTIC!"

That did it. "Oh, be quiet!" Lars told Anders and Tina. "You're not so great-looking yourself!"

Lars tried to pretend he didn't care. Instead, he wished he could sneak out and disappear into the woods. He felt miserable inside. *Why do kids always pick on me? I must be as clumsy looking as they think.*

At home, at Spirit Lake School, or at church, it was always the same. Kids took every chance they got to torment him.

But today his mother called a halt to the teasing. "Don't listen to them, Lars," she said. "Pretty soon you'll get your height. The rest of your body will catch up with your hands and feet."

Just the same, her words didn't comfort Lars. One picture stayed in his mind—the size of the great bear paw prints he had seen in the snow.

That evening Lars was still thinking about his new nickname. To make things even worse, he could remember every name that mean boys had ever called him. It didn't matter how long ago they had teased him. Their nicknames piled up, one on top of another.

Standing in front of the mirror in his bedroom, Lars stared at himself. *It's not just my hands and feet. My nose is too big, too.*

Just then he saw a picture of Anders tucked between the frame of the mirror and the glass. Taken at least three years before, the picture showed Anders ready to ride off on his horse, Wildfire. Anders was about the age Lars was now.

Looking at the picture more closely, Lars felt surprised. *His hands were just as big as mine! And his feet really do look like big bear paws! How come it didn't bother Anders?*

Dropping down on his bed, Lars lay there, staring up at the ceiling. It took a lot of thought, but at last something clicked in his mind. As though there were a picture holding the moment forever, Lars remembered a scene a few years ago.

A neighborhood boy named Stretch had spied the clunky boots Anders wore when cleaning out the barn. Long before, the boots had lost their shape and looked even bigger than the shoes Anders wore for school.

Stretch roared with laughter. "What big feet you have!" he said as though he were Little Red Riding Hood meeting the wolf.

"The better to kick you with!" Anders flipped back. Both of them laughed.

Thinking about it now, Lars couldn't remember another time Stretch teased Anders about the size of his feet.

I bet kids tease me because they know I can't take it, thought Lars.

In the days that followed, he worked hard at trying something new. At first it felt strange. He had a hard time coming up with funny answers instead of hurt feelings. Sometimes the moment was over before he figured out what to say. But when Anders called out, "Hey, you with the big feet!" Lars answered, "The better to kick you with!"

Anders looked at him and grinned. Then suddenly, as though he saw something new in Lars, Anders slapped him on the back.

From that time on, teasing was a game between them instead of something that hurt. And because he knew that Anders understood, Lars felt great right down to the toes of his bear paw clodhoppers.

TO **TALK** ABOUT

▶ Some kids get a reputation for teasing. Other kids get a reputation for being an easy mark. **If kids know you get upset, they'll think it's fun to pick on you.** What choice did Lars make about how he wanted to handle kids who teased him? How did he become an in-spite-of-it kid?

▶ **Sometimes it's important that you don't take yourself too seriously.** What's the difference between putting yourself down and laughing at yourself? Give examples from this story about Lars.

▸ A kid who always tries to be a clown may be covering up hurt. What's the difference between having kids laugh *at* you and laugh *with* you?

▸ Sometimes kids tease because they know someone like Lars can't take a joke. Other times kids tease because they know the person can take it and respond in a good way. How can you know if a kid is being mean when teasing you? How can you know if kids tease because they like and respect you? How does knowing that difference affect your self-esteem?

▸ If you like to tease others, how can you know when it's time to stop?

▸ There are some things that you *shouldn't* tease about at all. What are they? How can that kind of teasing seriously hurt a person?

▸ Sometimes teasing leads to a fight. Why are some things not worth a fight? Can it be a wise choice to walk away from a fight? Why or why not?

[God] will yet fill your mouth with laughter and your lips with shouts of joy. Job 8:21

Jesus, when kids tease me, I keep thinking about what they say and I feel terrible. Show me how to handle teasing. Help me so I don't take myself too seriously. If I need to, help me to even laugh at myself.

More Than Hot Lunch

Joy pushed her books into her locker and took off down the hall. Maybe she could manage to escape the kids if she left by a different door than usual.

But Kip must have been watching for her. As Joy tried to edge past a group of boys, he separated himself from the others and fell into step beside her.

"Joy, I'm sorry about what happened at lunch today," he said.

Joy remained silent.

"I'm sorry about what the other guys said."

Still Joy didn't speak, and Kip began looking uncomfortable.

"Hey, Joy, help me out. I'm apologizing."

"I accept your apology," she said, her voice soft but edged with hurt. "I forgive you."

"Then what's wrong? Forgive and forget, you know?"

Joy kept walking, gazing straight ahead. "I said I'd forgive you. I'll do my best to forget, but . . ."

"But what?"

Joy looked straight into Kip's eyes. "Where were you when I needed you?"

Kip's face flushed red. "You wanted me to speak up," he muttered.

"Yes, I wanted you to speak up." Suddenly Joy's mouth trembled—a warning that she was about to cry. Once again she looked straight ahead, walking faster.

"We talked about this," she said. "Remember? We made an agreement. Sunday night at church we both said we wanted to witness more at school."

She looked at Kip, and he nodded.

"So today I wore this little cross-and-heart pin on my collar. I knew kids would ask what it means. They always do. I prayed it would give me a chance to talk about Jesus. It did. I was having a good talk with Lisa until—"

"Until Cody came past with a tray," Kip finished for her. "Until Cody heard what you were talking about and brought the guys over."

"And you didn't back me up or even seem to agree with me. You didn't say one word!"

Now it was Kip's turn to look straight ahead. "Joy—"

"I've forgiven you, Kip." Again Joy's voice was quiet, but there was a new tone in it. "Where's the commitment you've been talking about? Did you mean what you said?"

Without another word, Joy turned and half walked, half ran the three blocks home. All she wanted was to reach her own room. As she shut the door, she tried to close out what had happened—the voices teasing her, calling her a Jesus freak; the laughter over what she'd said to Lisa; Kip just watching, saying nothing.

Joy's face burned hot thinking about how embarrassed she'd been. She wanted to cry. She wanted to be mad. She wanted to throw something. But most of all, she just hurt, way down inside.

Then she remembered Lisa. "She was listening, Lord. Lisa was listening until the boys started causing trouble. Will everything we talked about be wasted?"

Joy's shoulders started to shake, and the sobs came from the deepest part of her being. Picking up her Bible, she hugged it to herself as though she didn't know what else to do.

At last Joy opened the pages and turned to words she had memorized but needed to read: "I assure you that those who declare publicly that they belong to me, the Son of Man will do the same for them before the angels of God. But those who reject me publicly, the Son of Man will also reject them before the angels of God" (Luke 12:8–9, TEV).

For a long time Joy stared at the words. Then she repeated them to herself. Finally she drew a long, ragged breath, stood up, and looked out the window. From deep inside a smile welled up and reached her face.

TO **TALK** ABOUT

▸ What probably hurt Joy's self-esteem more—the teasing from the other kids or Kip's failure to speak up?

▸ **Remember David's battle with Goliath? David cared about the reputation of our living God. David wanted the whole world to know that it is God who saves us.** Joy is also an in-spite-of-it kid. She cares deeply about what other kids believe about Jesus. In spite of how kids treated her, she stuck to what she believed.

▸ Near the end of the story Joy received comfort. What clues tell you that even though she was hurt, she became stronger because of what happened?

▶ How do you think Jesus feels about Joy's efforts to witness? What do you think will happen the next time Joy talks with her friend Lisa?

▶ What do you think about Kip's failure to speak up? Why does Kip need to ask Jesus for forgiveness?

▶ Why is it important that you witness to your friends, even though you're afraid?

▶ Are there kids or grown-ups you'd like to tell about Jesus? Who are they? How can you pray for them?

▶ What kind of help does Jesus promise if you witness about Him, even when it's difficult? For clues see Luke 12:11–12.

But even if you should suffer for what is right, you are blessed. "Do not fear what they fear; do not be frightened." But in your hearts set apart Christ as Lord. Always be prepared to give an answer to everyone who asks you to give the reason for the hope that you have. 1 Peter 3:14–15

Jesus, I'm afraid of what other kids say. Yet I ask you to give me the Holy Spirit's power to tell others about you. If kids tease me, remind me how much you love me and how much you want them to know your love.

Piece of Cake!

On that sunny June morning, Casey could hardly wait to get to the beach. All through the winter she had thought about returning for a week of camp. Best of all, her cabin counselor from last year would be back. More than once Jessica had made Casey feel like a special person. She remembered their talks well.

"You're a special person in God's sight," Jessica told her one night as they talked about self-esteem. "He'll help you become all that you can be."

Now Jessica was one of the lifeguards. All through the activities of the morning and lunchtime, Casey looked forward to talking with her again.

This year I can swim to the raft, Casey thought. In her mind's eye she could see it well. The raft was in deep water, out beyond the ropes that kept the younger children in. It was part of growing up to swim to the raft and jump and dive off. Casey could hardly wait.

When the time finally came, she hurried into her swimsuit and down to the beach.

"Hi, Casey!" Jessica called to her.

While Casey told about her school year, Jessica listened

to every word. It was just as good seeing Jessica as Casey had hoped.

Soon other kids filled the wide expanse of beach, and Jessica welcomed each of them. As she explained the rules, she pointed to the raft out beyond the safety ropes for young swimmers. While Jessica guarded from a high lifeguard's chair on the beach, another lifeguard would watch from a rowboat closer to the raft.

"No one swims to the raft without passing a test first," Jessica said.

She told them what to do. "Walk far enough into the water to swim, but stay along the shore."

Jessica pointed to a nearby post. "Start there. Go across the front of the beach to that post." Again she pointed. "Without stopping, return to the first post. If you can swim that far without touching bottom, we'll let you go to the raft."

Piece of cake! thought Casey. Starting at the first post, she swam across the front of the beach. As she started back, she felt tired. Before long she was winded and needed to stop and stand up.

As soon as she drew in great gulps of air, Casey dropped onto her stomach again. A few minutes later she reached the final post. But Jessica was waiting.

"Go up on the beach, Casey," she said.

"I'm gonna be really upset if I can't go to the raft," Casey told her.

But Jessica paid no attention. Instead, she divided the kids into two groups. The boys and girls who passed the test paired off as swimming buddies. The rest waited on shore.

As she watched her friends start for the raft, Casey felt sick inside. When Jessica paired her with a girl two years younger, Casey became angry.

"I can swim better than Megan!" she told Jessica.

"If you can, you have to show me," Jessica said. "You haven't gone swimming all winter, have you?"

Scowling, Casey shook her head. In spite of what Jessica said, Casey wanted to be out on the raft, not swimming with a kid half her size.

"All your big talk about self-esteem!" she told Jessica. "If you really meant what you said last year, you'd let me prove myself. I'm ready for the raft!"

Jessica flushed but turned to the kids waiting on shore. "If one of you gets out of the water for some reason, you both get out. Okay? No swimming without a buddy."

For the first half hour Casey swam with Megan. When the younger girl left for the bathroom, Casey made up her mind.

Jessica's my friend. If I head for the raft, she won't stop me. In fact, she won't even know.

Passing quickly through the crowded part of the beach, Casey swam under the ropes. As she struck out for the raft, her swimming went well. Each time she looked up, she checked the distance. Closer. Closer. Closer. But she still had a way to go when she started feeling tired.

It wasn't long before her arms felt heavy. Soon Casey started gasping for air. *Can I make it?* Desperate now, she stretched down a leg. Unable to touch bottom, she panicked. Taking in a great gulp of water, she choked.

As she started to sink, she heard a sharp whistle. A voice through a megaphone. Oars dipping in water. Then a hand reached down, grabbing Casey under the arm.

A lifeguard pulled Casey next to the boat. "Hang on to the end of the boat," he said. "I'm taking you in."

Casey took two deep breaths. "I'm going to the raft."

"No, you're not."

When the boat reached the ropes, Jessica was waiting for Casey. "You're beached," Jessica said. "Wait up on shore for me."

When Casey walked out of the water, Megan stood on the sand.

"So you're the one who told on me!" Casey exclaimed.

Megan's eyes flashed. "I'm supposed to let you drown instead?"

Casey was really angry now. But when she turned around to stomp off, she found Jessica behind her.

"Megan stuck to the rules," Jessica said. "But I had already seen you. So had the other lifeguard. Did you even hear my whistle?"

Casey dug her toes into the sand. "I could have made it!"

Jessica shook her head. "No swimming the rest of the afternoon."

"What?" Casey glared at Jessica. "You gotta be kidding!"

"For the next three days you can swim along shore. On Thursday I'll test you again. Maybe you'll be ready for the raft. That is, if you don't bend the rules before then."

Casey stared at her. "I thought you were my friend!"

"I am," Jessica said. "Believe me, Casey, I am."

TO **TALK** ABOUT

▸ Do you think Jessica was Casey's friend? Give reasons for your answer.

▸ Have you ever been disappointed because you didn't get what you wanted? Describe what happened.

▸ Why is it important to follow rules? How did Casey try to take a shortcut around what was expected?

▸ What does it mean to bend the rules? What concerned Jessica most—Casey's self-esteem or her safety? How do you know?

▸ **All of us develop self-esteem by taking small steps. We learn what is needed, pass tests, and earn new privileges.** Will a kid who bends the rules have true self-esteem in that area? Why or why not?

▸ God likes to teach you step by step. If you learn according to His best plan for you, you'll go from doing easier things to harder. When He leads you on to the next step, you'll be prepared to do something more difficult. What privileges have you earned because you were willing to take the small steps?

▸ Did Jesus ever bend the rules to get what He wanted? How was He a person of integrity—a person who could be trusted to do what was right, even when there was a cost?

"There is nothing concealed that will not be disclosed, or hidden that will not be made known." Matthew 10:26 (TEV)

Thank you, Jesus, that you teach me step by step. Help me to be honest in each step so that I'm ready to go on to new privileges. Help me to have integrity—to do what is right even when you and I are the only ones who know about it.

159

He's My Brother

They had finished buying clothes for Darren when Mom asked the question. "Mike, will you and Darren go see the rock exhibit while I do my own shopping? It's in the other part of the mall."

Mike knew he couldn't say no. Long ago he'd learned that Mom needed help with Darren. Yet that didn't mean he *wanted* to do what she asked.

Grasping the handgrips, he swung Darren's wheelchair around. Carefully he steered through the narrow aisles between clothing displays. But his old question was back. *What if someone from school sees me?*

Three years older than Mike, Darren had always gone to a different school—one for kids with special needs. Darren had been born with cerebral palsy (sehr-ee-bruhl pall-zee). Because of the damage to his brain at birth or before, he often couldn't make his muscles do what he wanted.

As he looked down, Mike saw Darren's arm jerk out. He knew his brother couldn't help it any more than Darren could help being in a wheelchair. But his arm caught a pile of shirts on a nearby counter, dragging several of them onto the floor.

Inwardly Mike groaned. *Why do we always have to at-*

tract attention? Edging around the wheelchair, he started to pick up the shirts.

Off to the right a salesclerk turned toward them. "What are you doing?" she asked.

As Mike knelt down, the clerk came closer and saw Darren. "Oh, excuse me," she mumbled.

Darren started to speak. Mike knew Darren was trying to say he was sorry, but the clerk didn't wait to listen. Looking embarrassed about Darren's stumbling sounds, she gathered up an armload of shirts, dropped them on the counter, and hurried off.

Mike turned in time to see the hurt in Darren's eyes. Forcing himself to make the effort, he spoke. "It's okay, Darren."

Darren's mouth shaped a crooked smile. His words stumbled out. "Should I try it again?"

In spite of himself, Mike grinned. He also felt a bit ashamed. For the first time he wondered, *What if I were the one in the wheelchair?*

Soon they came to the rock and mineral show. A crowd had gathered, but Mike did his best to get Darren up front where he could see. For as long as Mike could remember, Darren had collected rocks. By now he owned over two hundred and knew the scientific name of each one.

Darren wanted to get closer to the geodes (jee-odes). Gray on the outside and shaped like a ball, they were cut open so people could see the colorful hollow at the center. Each hollow was lined with beautiful crystals.

Mike edged the wheelchair up to the table. The boy standing next to Darren looked down and moved slightly, giving him more room.

Mike froze. *Brad!* he thought. *The best football player in school!*

Quietly Mike moved away from Darren, thinking, *I hope Brad doesn't see me.*

Brad didn't. Soon he was talking with Darren. Both of them had noticed the same rock.

"Geode," Darren said, the word coming clearer than usual.

As he reached for the rock, his hand swung wildly and missed. He tried again. This time, as his hand came back, he picked up the geode. With an effort he turned it so Brad could see the crystals.

Mike couldn't hear what Brad said. But as he watched, Brad leaned down, listening carefully. A moment later he grinned and nodded his head.

Just then Brad looked up and saw Mike. He motioned for him to come over. "Come here. I want to show you something," he said. "It's just the rock I need for my collection."

"You collect rocks?" Mike asked.

"Yeah," answered Brad. "But I don't have very many." He nodded toward Darren. "He says he has two hundred. Mike, this is Darren."

For a moment Mike argued with himself. *I could pretend I'm not with him. I could get away with it.*

Then Mike tossed out the idea. "I know Darren," he said. "He's my brother."

When Darren's head jerked in his direction, Mike knew. Darren had caught something different in his voice.

Brad's eyes showed surprise. "Your brother?"

Deep inside, Mike realized that for the first time he'd accepted his brother just the way he was. "Yup," Mike said proudly. "He's my brother, and I'm glad."

TO **TALK** ABOUT

▸ Cerebral palsy makes it hard for people to make their muscles do what they want. How did cerebral palsy affect Darren's ability to walk, speak, pick up rocks, and other things?

▸ How do you think Darren felt about not being able to do the things he'd like?

▸ Why was Mike embarrassed about his brother's physical disability?

▸ Brad gave Darren some very special gifts. What were they?

▸ Why was it important to Darren's self-esteem that Mike chose to accept him just the way he was?

▸ What happened to Mike's feelings when he told Brad that Darren was his brother? Why was it important to Mike's self-esteem that he accepted Darren as he was?

▸ **Often people with physical, emotional, or intellectual disabilities work very hard to develop their full potential. Often they reach their goals and succeed in amazing ways.** What does it mean to say that a person developed to his or her full potential?

▸ Cerebral palsy affects people in a variety of ways, depending on the amount of brain damage. Some people are very limited in their physical activities. Others are not. Do you know anyone who has cerebral palsy or another kind of physical disability? What kind of things are they able to do, in spite of their disability? How can you help them?

[Jesus said,] "In everything, do to others what you would have them do to you." Matthew 7:12a

Jesus, often I don't know how to act around people who can't do all the things I can. Help me accept them the way they are so I'm free to love them. Help me to help them be all they can be.

A Phone
of My Own

It all started in school that day. Kayla's friend Dakota had just gotten her own phone and private number. And Shannon came to school with a great new jacket—the kind Kayla always wanted.

Listening to her friends talk, she wondered, *Why can't I have the things they have?*

All afternoon Kayla thought about it. By the time she left for home, she'd convinced herself. *I'll start with a phone. Maybe if I wear Mom down by asking enough times, she'll give in.*

When Kayla opened the door, her mother was in the kitchen fixing supper. At Mom's feet, two-year-old Hannah played on the floor. Around Hannah lay all the pots and pans she had taken from the cupboard.

Mom gave Kayla a hug. "Have a good day?"

Kayla nodded as though she really hadn't heard Mom's question.

At the kitchen table her little brother, Johnnie, was coloring a picture. Proudly he held it up for Kayla to see, but she barely noticed. Instead, she launched her attack.

"Dakota's dad gave her a phone of her own."

Mom pushed the hair out of her eyes. "Kayla, we've talked about this before."

"But I want to talk about it again. She has the phone in her room and her own private number."

"Dakota's dad gets business calls at home," answered Mom. "He can't afford to have her tie up the phone."

"But if I had one, I could talk as long as I wanted."

Instead of answering, Mom started to peel the potatoes.

"I could talk without everyone listening," Kayla added.

As she watched, her mother's shoulders sagged slightly. *I'm getting through,* she thought. *I'll wear her down, all right.*

But in that moment Mom turned from the sink. "Even if we had the money, it wouldn't be good for you."

"Why not?" Kayla asked.

Mom sighed, and the tired lines around her eyes seemed deeper. "Kayla, have you heard yourself talk lately? 'I want, I want, I want.'"

"Yes, I want this," answered Kayla, her voice filled with resentment. "If you wanted to give it to me, you could. You just don't love me enough."

"I love you so much I don't want you to be selfish," Mom said, her voice firm. "You need to know how to share the phone with the rest of us."

"Aw, Mom."

"The answer is no."

Kayla ran to her room and didn't come out until supper. Except for saying "hi" to Dad, she was silent. All through supper her anger simmered. Even when little Hannah threw her plate on the floor, Kayla sat unmoved, her face stony.

As Mom cleaned up the mess, she looked as if she was going to cry. But Kayla pretended she didn't see.

Later that evening Kayla plopped down in front of the TV. Dad was watching a special on public television.

"Who is she?" Kayla asked as she saw a tiny woman wearing a long white robe-like dress.

"Mother Teresa," Dad answered. "A woman who gave her life to help the poor and dying in India."

Kayla groaned. "Can't we watch something else?"

"I want to see this," said Dad. "Your turn next—if there's something good."

Kayla waited, hoping the program would be over soon. On the screen a young woman described Mother Teresa. "Mother said she wanted to die on her feet. I think that's just what she did. She gave herself to the last drop."

Stupid way to live, thought Kayla.

But then the program showed footage of the small woman. Her white clothing was edged with a blue border, and her skin held deep lines. Something in her face caught Kayla's attention.

As Mother Teresa bowed her head in prayer, Kayla listened and remembered one sentence: "It is by forgetting self that one lives."

Suddenly Kayla had a strange feeling. She wished she could have whatever it was Mother Teresa had. In spite of her tiny size, there was something very big about her. For some reason she seemed happy inside, even though she lived among the poor in India.

All evening Kayla tried to forget Mother Teresa's prayer. Instead, the sentence stayed in Kayla's mind. *What does it mean to forget about myself so that I live?*

Kayla tried to push the question away, but the pictures in her memory wouldn't leave. She thought of the streets of India and how she had bugged Mom for a phone of her own.

She remembered the hunger and rags, and then her own desire for another jacket. As much as she wanted to forget the starving bodies she'd seen, she could not erase them from her mind.

For the first time in over a year, Kayla thought about the choice she'd made when she was nine years old. Back then she had prayed, "Jesus, I want my life to count for you. I want to tell others about your love."

Now Kayla felt ashamed. She'd avoided God for so long; it felt strange to talk with Him. Yet Kayla knew she would dislike herself even more if she didn't.

"Forgive me, Jesus, for always wanting things. Forgive me for always thinking about myself. Show me how I can help others."

When Kayla finished praying, it felt as if a bag filled with heavy stones had fallen off her back. Crawling into bed, she slipped between clean sheets and pulled a handmade quilt around her shoulders.

As she nestled down, Kayla suddenly knew how to begin. *Mom and Dad would like going out for breakfast Saturday morning. I'll offer to baby-sit Hannah and Johnnie.*

Drifting off to sleep, Kayla felt as if she might even like herself again.

TO **TALK** ABOUT

▸ How do you think Kayla felt about herself when she kept asking for things? How does selfishness destroy self-esteem?

▸ When did Kayla's selfish feelings change? Why?

▸ What does it mean to deny yourself? Does it mean to hide

your good qualities and personality? Or to put away selfish wishes? Which do you think Jesus wants you to do?

▸ Kayla became an in-spite-of-it kid because she chose to love and help others. How did she start letting God use her right away? How will that kind of growing help her when she gets older?

▸ Are there ways in which you've been selfish? What are some practical ways you can reach out to help other people?

▸ **While Jesus was here on earth, He showed us a servant's heart.** How did Jesus act? What *is* a servant's heart? For clues see John 13:1–17.

▸ If you choose to serve others, how will it change your life? Why?

[Jesus said,] "If anyone would come after me, he must deny himself and take up his cross daily and follow me." Luke 9:23

"Everything is possible for him who believes." Mark 9:23b

Forgive me, Jesus, for just thinking about myself and what I want. Help me live the way you did when you were here on earth. In your name I choose to follow you without any excuses about what I can't do. I choose to deny myself and serve you.

Thank you, Jesus, for being the God of the impossible. Thank you that you will help me do whatever you want me to do. I praise your holy name!

For In-Spite-of-It Kids

Remember David and how he picked up five stones from the creek? He didn't need more than one for killing Goliath. Yet he had other stones as backup—just in case.

While reading this book, you may have needed only one idea to bring down an enemy of your self-esteem. But you may have picked up several more ideas—just in case. Have you also discovered how often you need to make a choice?

Learning to see yourself as God sees you takes time. Whenever you believe you're a valuable person in His sight, you pick up a stone. You put aside enemy thoughts. You start forming the habit of letting God love you. It's like letting your mom or dad give you a hug.

If your self-esteem is based on God's love and forgiveness, you know you can trust Him. Even though you don't understand why some things happen, you believe that Jesus is bigger than your problems. You learn that the Holy Spirit helps you with your daily battles.

David didn't trust in what he could do. David trusted God and knew what God could do. You have the same privilege. **When you know Jesus and belong to Him, He helps**

you face giants. In the heat of battle, you learn to depend on Him.

In whatever you face in the days and years ahead, keep your eyes on Jesus. In everything you do and for as long as you live, He is the audience you care about.

Hebrews 13:5–6 gives God's promise for you: **"I will never leave you nor forsake you."** Therefore you may boldly say: **"The Lord is my helper; I will not fear. What can man do to me?"** (NKJV)

With your hand in the hand of God, you're worth more than you think!

Acknowledgments

My gratitude to the Lord
and these other builders of my self-esteem:

My husband, Roy
Kevin Johnson and Cliff Bjork
Pat Rosenberg
Jeff Boyum
Jerry Foley, Penny Stokes, and Terry White
Charette Barta and Traci Mullins
Jeanne Mikkelson
Rochelle Glöege, Natasha Sperling,
and the entire Bethany team